BE *Held* BY *Him*
COMPANION GUIDEBOOK

SOME REAL PEOPLE'S RESPONSES ABOUT THE GUIDEBOOK...

Karen's guidebook invites you, the reader, to "Find God When Life Knocks You Off Your Feet." It is not just a journal; it's a roadmap that leads you on an exciting journey of discovery. Karen doesn't just talk about finding God, she offers a myriad of fresh new ideas and creative approaches that have inspired me to rethink, re-examine and recharge my own relationship with Him.

Karen's guidebook is for everyone who has ever struggled to find God amid pain and hardship, for those who cry out "Yes, but HOW" when the best advice they can find is to press into God, for those who know He is out there "somewhere," but are not quite sure where to look, how to recognize His voice, or how to just yield to His comforting presence in the middle of the furnace.

With the refreshing insight that comes from her own place of pain, and with the wisdom gleaned from years spent searching, listening, and then submitting, Karen offers the fellow traveller a way through.

– Julie Jones

Karen, I love, love, LOVE the guidebook!

This is why: through my years of being in church, I would hear statements like "Walk with God," but it never went any farther. I was never really told how to walk with God.

Well, I just found the book that tells a person how to walk with God. It is just fabulous. If the reader followed what you say step by step, I feel sure the person would have a wonderful walk with God. Oh, yes, that's why I need to go through it!

You have done Christians a big favor with writing this series.

– Linda Stubblefield

I have had the privilege of knowing Karen for some years as a lover of God and a woman of prayer. This book and its companion guidebook hold so many practical and creative keys to walking through life's difficulties, keeping God as the focus, whether or not our personal challenges are similar to Karen's. Her testimonies, like those in the Bible itself, are real "rubber hits the road" stuff; she doesn't try to sugarcoat any of the struggles. But a mark of Karen's walk with the Lord is that she asks great questions of Him and knows Him well enough to listen for and expect His life-giving responses—not because she is any "more favoured" than the rest of us, but because she knows the Lord loves to have two-way conversations with His children (and that's really what prayer is all about).

– Sue Otto

I am so thankful for Karen's beautiful heart and the way God speaks through her in this guidebook. As a fellow sufferer navigating the world of "mysterious illnesses," soaking up the Lord's rest and peace through these thoughts and encouragements helps the pain to fade, giving me the ability to truly rest in the Father, focus on Jesus, and feel the closeness of Holy Spirit.

While I too wish I had this book ten years ago, I know without a shadow of a doubt that God's timing is always good, so I am thankful to have it right now—today.

I encourage you to take time to get away with the Lord. Go on this journey together and experience His peace, love, joy, faithfulness, goodness and all the rest of His spiritual fruit. It is all here with Him, waiting for you to join in. Like me, I know you will be glad you did.

– Shannon Spencer, Business Coach
Founder of the Savvy Woman Christian Business Network
ShannonSpencerConsulting.com

Karen's book is like a friend, holding your hand and leading you to sweet communion with your Heavenly Father.

She shares her experience, along with Scripture and practical exercises to lead the reader into healthy thinking and living. There are no "shoulds" in this book—only compassion, love, and hope.

Karen's book is not only an honest sharing of her battle with physical and emotional pain but also a testimony of our Lord's great love for His children. She shares how through her pain He worked, loved and held her close. As he wants to do for each of us.

– Anna Hoffman

BOOK 1

BE Held BY Him
COMPANION GUIDEBOOK

KAREN BROUGH
Written by a very natural girl and a supernatural God

THE HOLY BIBLE, NEW INTERNATIONAL VERSION®, NIV® Copyright © 1973, 1978, 1984, 2011 by Biblica, Inc.® Used by permission. All rights reserved worldwide.

Scripture quotations marked NLT are taken from the *Holy Bible*, New Living Translation, copyright © 1996, 2004, 2015 by Tyndale House Foundation. Used by permission of Tyndale House Publishers, Inc., Carol Stream, Illinois 60188. All rights reserved.

Scripture taken from the New King James Version®. Copyright © 1982 by Thomas Nelson. Used by permission. All rights reserved.

The ESV® Bible (The Holy Bible, English Standard Version®). ESV® Text Edition: 2016. Copyright © 2001 by Crossway, a publishing ministry of Good News Publishers. The ESV® text has been reproduced in cooperation with and by permission of Good News Publishers. Unauthorized reproduction of this publication is prohibited. All rights reserved.

NASB New American Standard Bible®, Copyright © 1960, 1971, 1977, 1995, 2020 by The Lockman Foundation. All rights reserved.

Scripture quotations marked TPT are from The Passion Translation®. Copyright © 2017, 2018, 2020 by Passion & Fire Ministries, Inc. Used by permission. All rights reserved.

ThePassionTranslation.com. Holman Christian Standard Bible® Copyright © 1999, 2000, 2002, 2003, 2009 by Holman Bible Publishers. Used with permission by Holman Bible Publishers, Nashville, Tennessee. All rights reserved.

The Holy Scriptures Jubilee Bible 2000 (JUB) Copyright © 2013, 2020 Translated and Edited by Russell M. Stendal NET Bible® copyright ©1996-2017 All rights reserved.

Build 30170414 by Biblical Studies Press, L.L.C. Copyright © 1995, 2003, 2013, 2014, 2019, 2020 by God's Word to the Nations Mission Society. All rights reserved.

The Holy Bible, Berean Study Bible, BSB Copyright ©2016, 2020 by Bible Hub Used by Permission. All Rights Reserved Worldwide.

Copyright © 2021 By Karen Brough
writtenbygodsgirl.com

Disclaimer: Although this publication is designed to provide accurate information in regard to the subject matter covered, the publisher and the author assume no responsibility for errors, inaccuracies, omissions, or any other inconsistencies herein. This publication is meant as a source of valuable information for the reader, however it is not meant as a replacement for direct expert assistance. If such level of assistance is required, the services of a competent professional should be sought.

All rights reserved. No part of this publication may be reproduced or transmitted in any form or by any means, electronic or mechanical, including photocopy, recording, or any information storage retrieval system, without permission in writing from the copyright owner.

978-0-6452451-4-1 (paperback edition)

*Dedicated to those who have always wanted to
walk with God but never knew how.*

*And to the brave ones, the creative ones,
the ones who need a fresh injection of hope
and connection with their Creator.*

This is for you precious ones.

xxxxx

THANKFEST

Thankyou to Father God, who has proven Himself my Rock, my Safe Place, my Loving Friend and Confidant more times than I can express, You are relentless in Your love of me, for that, I am so incredibly thankful.

Thankyou for Your inspiration and wisdom, Your dreams, ideas and visions for these books. I love creating with You – let's never stop.

xxxxx

To my dearest friends Julie, Deborah and Jane, your help in proofreading has been a gift greater than you'll ever know. Thankyou chickadees.

And to those ones who brought His love to me along the way:
You are more precious than you know.
More loved than I could ever hope to put into words.
And more valuable because of who you are, not what you do.
Sending you many hugs today and all days.

Thankyou.
xxxxx

EDITOR

(The ultimate language artist, accomplished, generous, and precious new friend from across the oceans)

Linda Stubblefield | affordablechristianediting.com

GRAPHIC CONCEPT DESIGN

(The intuitive, talented creative heart and developer of dreams)

Abigail Parker | abigail@sponge.com.au

MAP ILLUSTRATOR

(The courageous, gifted, illustrative visionary and Holy Spirit led, heart woman of His)

Stacey Leitch | staceyleitch.com

BOOK COVER DESIGN & FORMATTING

(The oh so patient, professional, full of integrity, skilled book creative and design king)

Steve Kuhn | kuhndesigngroup.com

Contents

Foreword 15

Preface 19

A Personal Letter to My Reader 21

Map 22

Book Elements 27

Where it all Began 29

1. Rest: *What to Do When You Can't Do Anything* 35
2. Be Still: *One Solution to a Racing Mind* 55
3. Giving and Receiving: *But Needy Is Hard, Lord* 73
4. Atmosphere: *Your Environment Can Change You* 91
5. Never Alone: *Isolation Is a Lie* 109
6. Safe Places and Safe People: *Worthy of Safety* 127
7. Trust: *Dare to Trust Again* 145
8. Kindness: *Be Kind to Myself* 161
9. God's Character: *God's Nature and Heart* 181
10. Listening: *Opening the Ears of My Heart* 199
11. God's Presence: *Life Is More than What Is Seen* 217
12. Prayer: *Developing Awareness of God in the Everyday* .. 235
13. Weakness: *When I Am Weak, He Is Strong* 257
14. Small Things: *Valuing the Small Builds the BIG* 279
15. Practical Survival Tips: *Life Checks and Balances* 297
16. Village Life: *Community—A Little Piece of Heaven* 315

APPENDICES

Appendix 1: Rest 335

Appendix 2: Village Life 339

Appendix 3: Safe Places, Safe People 347

Appendix 4: Be Kind to Myself 349

Appendix 5: Listening Foundations 351

Appendix 6: Life checks and balances 353

For Those on a Spiritual Journey Who Want to Connect
with God for Themselves 359

About the Author 363

Foreword

Ever since Karen mentioned to me she was writing a book, I've been excited to get my hands on it. Karen has immense moral authority when it comes to writing about the content this book addresses. She is a true overcomer in the face of adversity and ongoing crisis. Even if you do not share Karen's faith, there is something beautiful to read here.

Anyone who knows Karen would attest she is a very genuine, open, and authentic woman. Having demonstrated consistently over time an ability to live from a place of peace, despite her extraordinary and prolonged health crisis, means Karen is a voice worth listening to.

You see, I have known Karen for over fifteen years. In fact, I first met Karen when she was referred to see me from another local chiropractic practice. Karen's clinical presentation and health history were complex. Simply put, her body was a mess. She was in a health crisis. Even though I have assessed thousands of patients over the last 20 years, Karen's initial examination results are amongst those I still vividly recall. They don't stand out because they were good.

As a practitioner, I have seen my fair share of people in crisis. What fascinated me from my earliest years in practice, was trying to understand why some people are able to rise above their crisis, while others are overwhelmed by it. I had observed that people with a faith background tended to fare better. But not always.

Even after only a handful of consultations, I remember being impressed with how sincere Karen was about her faith. I was encouraged that such a belief system may help her navigate the future that may lay ahead. However, I had some concerns. There was no doubt that to Karen, the existence of a miracle-breathing God was real. Unfortunately, given the reality of her medical condition, it seemed to me that Karen's medical condition and belief system were on a collision course.

I was afraid I was about to witness a train wreck. I had sadly seen this sort of thing play out before.

My concern for Karen was simple. Her condition and situation were not likely to improve; if that proved to be the case, would it eventually trigger a crisis of faith? How would she respond once she realized her 'miracle breathing God' was not providing her a miracle? Would Karen lose hope in her God? If so, would the trauma of a faith crisis further accelerate her downward health spiral?

In any case, it appeared to me that based on her health information alone, there would be tough days ahead.

What was perhaps unknown to Karen and her health care team back then, was how much further her health would deteriorate. Indeed, her crisis deepened significantly. Insidiously, Karen completely lost her ability to work. Both her career and volunteering came to a grinding halt. Karen lost her ability to be active, socialize or even get out of the house. She would go on to experience multiple whole body collapses. It was evident to all that chronic disease was painfully and progressively stealing the best years of life away from this beautiful, intelligent, and caring woman.

This high-achieving woman and dedicated mother could no longer function. Period. Her former life stopped. Completely.

From a practitioner's perspective, Karen's story was in the top 1% of all clinical nightmares. It was a never-ending cycle of debilitating illness punctuated by excruciatingly painful flare-ups and a merry-go-round of doctor's appointments. As with many people with chronic health conditions, Karen suffered for a long time before getting a proper diagnosis. Sadly, once the diagnosis was established, Karen was confronted

FOREWORD

with the reality that while her condition was diagnosable, it was not medically curable. There was no 'wonder pill.' No magic bullet. No special diet. Nothing.

It is precisely this point that makes Karen's book so powerful and relevant.

Karen's journey is one of victory, like few people ever experience. It is not just about a deeply personal struggle with serious health issues. It is the lived experience of one who has overcome a crisis, even when the crisis is still ongoing. It is a story of finding peace, fulfillment, joy, and hope, even when your circumstances scream that it is impossible to do so. Even when you believe in miracles and no miracle of healing arrives.

What could be more relevant today than the real and personal experience of another human being who has faced a crisis and overcome, despite the crisis not ever going away?

Karen's book is not an account of her sickness. It is not a depressing read about one person's battle with failing health. It is not about her suffering. There is no chronological story telling from front to back cover. It is much more than that. Rather, it is almost as if Karen has generously opened up to us the most private pages in her guidebook and drawn out the nuggets of universal truth that have strengthened and encouraged her. Truths that have transformed her during, and even despite, her crisis.

It is a deep dive of discovery into the essence of what it means to be a human being. Karen has been vulnerable and brave. Raw and real. She has not held back. She has done more than just share her personal insights and reflections. She has provided us a road map based on her lived experience. A road map we can apply on our own journey of discovery to finding peace, fulfillment, joy, and hope. Even when life hurts.

This book is a wonderful resource. I would encourage you to read it the way it has been intended. Sit and ponder a chapter at a time. Even just part of a chapter. The book has been designed to choose the order in which you read the chapters, feel free to skip about in the book, allow yourself to be encouraged, uplifted, challenged, and stirred.

Unlike Karen, your crisis may not be a health crisis. Yours might be financial. Or relational. Or mental. Maybe your life has been interrupted by tragedy or an unexpected accident. Perhaps a loved one has been torn from you. You may have suffered abuse, isolation, or judgment. Whatever the case, this book is relevant to you. Karen has skillfully lifted the gems of truth from her own experience and has presented them to us here in a kindly and caring manner. What she shares is relevant to us no matter what crisis we face.

Perhaps your personal crisis hasn't even hit yet. Then all the better. You are in a wonderful and privileged position to dive into this book. Why wait for a crisis to discover greater meaning and richness in life.

One thing is sure, if you live long enough, you will experience your own personal crisis. Hopefully, yours is limited to a season in your life. Hopefully, yours ends in a miracle. Whatever the case will be for you, when your crisis comes, be encouraged that there will be a way forward.

This book makes a wonderful contribution to the understanding of how to transition from living as a "human doing" to becoming a completely fulfilled "human being." Karen authentically demonstrates that when you discover the richness of what it means to be a human being, being one is wonderful, despite your circumstance.

Karen's authentic life has touched me, my staff, and other patients. Despite her own serious medical battles, she has found the energy to write many kind, encouraging, inspired, and insightful personal notes to us over the years. I am now thrilled she has offered up this book into the public domain, where she shares with us openly the source of her strength. May this book enrich you in the way that Karen enriches those that know her.

Dr. Norman Craig Nelson
Chiropractor
BAppSc(ClinSc)/BChiropracticSc

Preface

Are you stressed, sick, worn out, or weary? Has your body broken, slowed up, or let you down?

Has life tossed you into unfamiliar waters, and you are struggling to find a place to land?

Do you feel out of control—at the whim of whatever comes at you, longing for something secure and unchanging to grab a hold of?

To feel "normal" again?

Have you ever felt that the situation you are facing is bigger than what you have the capacity to meet?

Do you feel as if you've nothing left to give, no ability to "push through" anymore?

Do you ever wonder where your peace and hope have gone, asking whether they're in hiding or have disappeared altogether?

> DO YOU FEEL ALONE IN ALL THAT YOU ARE WALKING THROUGH?

Do you feel alone in all that you are walking through?

Have you ever thought, "Where are You, God? Why is this happening to me?"

Are you struggling to hear, see or connect with God?

Have you ever wanted to experience Him tangibly? To see and feel His miraculous touch, to hear His loving voice, to sit with Him in the barbed times of life, and have your wounds tended by Him?

If you've asked any or all of these questions, you're in good company, and this companion guidebook is for you.

This is the book I needed ten years ago when I was struck with a debilitating mystery illness. Floundering for the first few months, I eventually realized that I needed God's help; the only way forward was with Him.

My offering is not intended to be a definitive final work on how and who God is; rather, a journey of one woman's encounter with Him in the hard places of tough seasons. Sharing the encouragements, wisdom He poured out to me in these times, hoping they will speak to and reassure you as well, in your own challenges. A collection of activations, ideas and inspiration for those new or old in faith – wanting the MORE of God we've always heard about.

In seasons of life, increasing numbers of people find themselves facing fatigue and health breakdown. Stressors and trouble pile one upon another with minimal recovery time. Have you noticed it too? Have you felt it yourself?

The pace of life events, traumas, sicknesses have sought to push us away

- From our peace
- From one another
- From intimacy with God
- From the very things that would help us in these times.

The need to connect with the One who knows the way forward is essential to survive and thrive through whatever life throws at us—choosing to look through His lens rather than my limited vision.

Learning how to hear and see His heart for my circumstance brings a whole other level of hope. I don't know about you, but I *need* His vision so much, especially when life throws me into deep waters.

If we are to have hope and help in our hour of need, we need to know how to hear and recognize God's voice—not because we *should* do it but because we *get to*. His voice is worth listening to, and His heart brings us good at this time—every time.

As you read this book, you will be:

- Tended to by His loving words
- Reassured that you are not alone in your pain, grief, or trouble
- Encouraged that others have gone before you and survived
- Lighter, with seeds of hope planted deep within you
- Experiencing His helping, healing hand at work in the everyday moments of your life
- Observing the ordinary becoming extraordinary as you become more aware of Him
- Aware of His redemptive plans and purposes, reigniting hope within you
- Uplifted as you develop a greater connection to Father God and recognize the loving tones of His voice

I needed these helps when all seemed confusing, hopeless, and overwhelming. So much mystery surrounded the present and the future, and I felt despair as a result. As time wore on, I understood that I was unwilling to live without hope, and the only place I found lasting hope was with Him. The only way forward was to allow God to carry me through these initial stages of life's upheaval.

Go on a journey together with Him. He won't load you down with more burdens but instead, lighten the load you already carry, healing and tending to raw spaces along the way.

Come. Come and be encouraged by God and all that He has done. Be uplifted, knowing that what He does for one, He can do for you and more.

LETTER TO THE READER

Dear Precious One Walking through a Tough Season,

I'm so excited for this coming season for you—when you have recovered enough to want to take action or are choosing to engage despite it—taking time to think, to ponder ideas and adventure with Him using this guidebook.

He doesn't require you to 'do,' but I'm thankful that you are up to doing anything. Please don't feel the need to rush through this guidebook as you would an assignment. This guidebook contains years' worth of living out. If you take a little time to travel through it with Him, that's definitely okay.

Let this be the first guidebook you practice, pray and communicate personally with the Father of your heart. Not because you feel you have to, but because you get to.

You might notice the autumn leaf on the cover looks a little different from the testimony (being) book. I felt God show me how through the guidebook, we have the opportunity to come closer to Him.

Where in the 'being' book, we are able to observe from afar, this guidebook aims to be a 'doing' book. A resource to put legs on this God adventure amid your own tough time.

It's intention is to freshly inspire connection to God, whether it's a brand new relationship or decades long faith journey, I pray that this companion guidebook blesses you greatly. As the process of living it out and writing it has me.

My personal desire and prayer is for you to connect with God in the deep, satisfying and fun relational way which He has prepared for each one of us.

God bless you dearly, precious one of His.

I pray that you are encouraged, inspired and excited to spend time, connect and converse with Him who loves you most.

Much love,
Karen
xxxxx

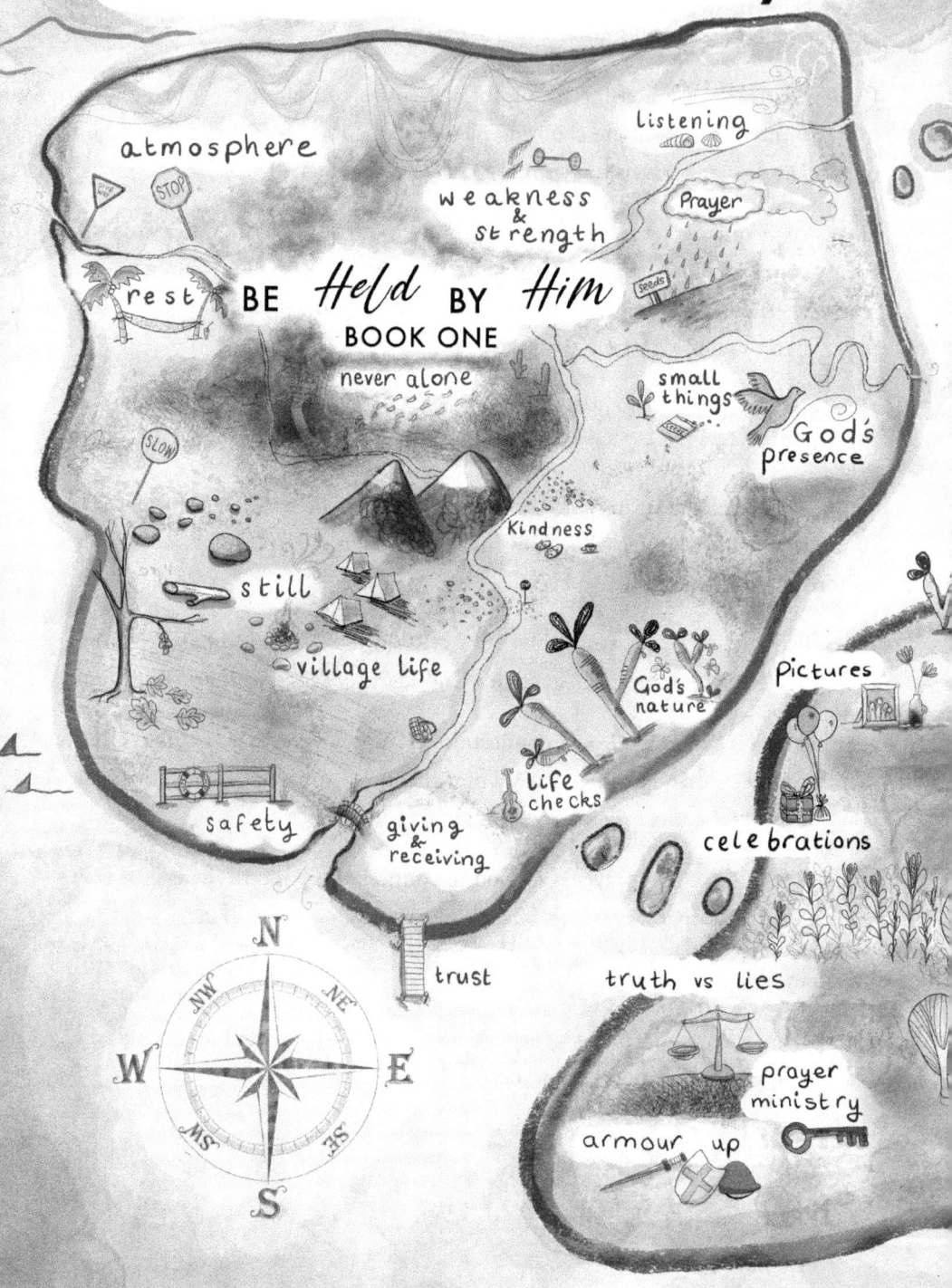

EXPLANATION OF THE MAP

'The Journey' map outlines the various chapters of each book in the 'Be Held by Him' series.

Rather than list off the chapter topics, the precious Mindy Kirker 'Flourish writers' suggested an infographic map might be effective in covering the content of the three books in one. It felt as if air came into my lungs when she suggested this God inspired idea. Thankyou Mindy!

Not long after this, God gave me a dream, revealing the three stages of health/capacity, when hardship hits. He revealed there were three islands, and just as I did, my reader would move from a desert like experience to places of flourish with Him.

Finally, through another dream, and a few recommendations from people in the dream, He brought across my path the gifted illustrator, Stacey Leitch. She understood the subject matter personally and the moment we spoke, I knew she would be the right person for the work.

She has created this prophetic artwork based on the book chapters and content. We've brainstormed and she's brought the conversations, God's instruction and her vision into something that continues to speak to me daily. God bless you and your gift Stacey.

'The Journey' reveals a story of how God speaks to and interacts with us, especially in the hard seasons of life. I've thoroughly enjoyed the detailed gifts of hope Stacey has helped communicate through the map and more than that, revealed Father's heart for us in the tough.

I pray it encourages you & invests hope in you.

There is always so much more to look forward to, with God by your side. Don't give up!

INSIDE THIS BOOK, YOU WILL FIND EACH OF THESE ELEMENTS.

1. A Key Name

2. Take Aways

Revelations/wisdom/teaching points for those who can't absorb a lot of information or need to get straight to the point.

3. Questions to Ponder

For personal reflective time with God.

4. Journal Space

Write any thoughts, ideas, revelations, and insights.

5. Playlist

Inspirational songs to soak, worship, declare, inspire.

6. Activations/Applications

Choose one or all activations. We are not all designed to connect with God in the same way, this is the place to try some new ways or revisit the old. Loosely based on Gardener's multiple intelligences.

7. Blessing

Receive the blessings you need and want, let the others remain on the shelf for later, or gift it to someone else.

THIS COMPANION GUIDEBOOK IS A DOING BOOK.

A collection of ways God connected with and encouraged me following this health event.

It's His wisdom – the one-liners which reframed my thinking, situation and often changed an entire day.

The songs and verses which shifted atmospheres.

And the activations which invested hope and tangible encounters with our Mighty God, Loving Jesus, and Empowering Holy Spirit.

The journey map will be a guide—ways God can speak and connect with all of us at any time. It covers the three books in the series and their chapters. It endevours to invest hope, if you are in a desert space right now. Take heart, there is more goodness to come!

When everything felt disconnected and battles raged, as I searched for purpose, hope and identity – these are the ways He made Himself known to me. These are also the ways I chose to reach up to Him and invite Him into my mystery.

Relationship is a two-way street, and my hope is that this book develops greater intimacy between you and Father God.

That He'll inspire you, tend to you, meet you powerfully-as you choose to reach out and interact with the One who knows all that you walk through, and wants to bring you hope, purpose, light in life, and faith like you've not experienced before.

Much love
Karen
xxxxx

A WORD OF WARNING

The following is my personal "beginning" health story that could contain some triggering aspects for those in raw places.

If you are in this place, you may want to consult the contents page for a chapter that speaks directly to your heart.

WHERE IT ALL BEGAN

Lying upon the bed, unable to move my limbs, head, and body, my heart wept. *Am I dying? Is this IT? What about my hubby Craig and the kids?* Thoughts were racing in and out, endeavoring to find a place to land, to find order and explanation…but at that moment, there was none to find.

The constant headache of the past six weeks hadn't slowed me up; I pushed through, taking paracetamol to try and ease the knifelike pangs, to no avail. I pushed on, meeting the commitments, the pressures of being a wife, a mum, a business partner, a teacher, the various voluntary committees, responsibilities, and relationships—everything cried out for more—of me. That small voice within screamed for me to slow down, but in my mind, there was simply no time…

No time to stop…

No time to consider and ask what was causing the unfamiliar symptom…

No time to cull the calendar craziness…

No time to be still…

No time…

No time…

No time…

"It'll have to wait" was a common thought of this time, prioritizing everyone else but myself. Sacrificing myself for others, that's what real service is about, isn't it? I was a servant-hearted wife of one, the mother of three, and now I couldn't do a thing.

My body had sent out the warning signs—the unheeded flashing red lights trying their best to let me know things weren't right. I hadn't listened, and now, I'd pushed it beyond its limits. Layer upon layer of the past year's stresses flooded to mind as I lay there, waiting for the ambulance to arrive.

Pale, exhausted, unable to lift a single finger, I was at the whim of life and circumstances. My body had had enough! I now had no choice; my body would take what it needed—with or without my permission.

So, I lay there, so filled with weakness that nothing would function as I willed it to—as fear expanded within.

Terror seized my distress, and they embraced.

As the seconds passed, new symptoms appeared, and I felt as though life was leaving me. My eyes closed, and I tried desperately to come to peace with what I was leaving behind.

My family, oh, my precious family—Craig, my children.

Just moments before, in our first extended family dinner in months, we had been busy catching up around the dinner table. Everyone was able to be there; what a delight! So good to be back at the family home.

Squeals of joy came from our kids and their cousins as they played happily in the background. Mum and Dad were in the kitchen cleaning up, and my sister and I bantered back and forth across the table, having some good hearty laughs. These times were precious. My family was so dear to me. Together is the place I wanted to be all the time. These nights were a balm for my soul.

Then in a split second, everything changed.

My eyes began to move of their own accord as if some mysterious fingers were pulling the muscles behind them. My neck became sore, stiff, and the slight headache intensified.

My body felt the waves of nausea and fatigue HIT, and boy, did it hit! Any energy I had dissipated and withdrew, heading who knows where. Beginning with my extremities, I felt as if my blood was retreating. My hands weakened, and my arms fell limply to the sides of my body. My head joined the procession and dropped upon my shoulder. The weightiness of it propelled my immobilized body to the right—where Craig sat.

"Catch me, honey," I barely breathed out as my entire body fell upon his lap.

Apart from the sheer physical exhaustion and my brain feeling as though it was splitting in two, I don't remember much of the following minutes. My listless, unresponsive form was carried to my parent's bedroom nearby, and an ambulance was called.

Time stood still, and I couldn't comprehend much of what anyone was saying. Every cell of my body felt weighty—sleepy, as if the energy had been sucked out of every molecule. They demanded rest, and rest they did.

The medical staff arrived, and the family tension was relieved on some level for a moment. The cavalry had arrived, and now they could "fix" Karen.

> MY BODY HAD HAD ENOUGH! I NOW HAD NO CHOICE; MY BODY WOULD TAKE WHAT IT NEEDED—WITH OR WITHOUT MY PERMISSION.

They took my vitals and eventually surmised that I was "…just a tired Mum" as they offered to take me into the hospital but articulating that they wouldn't do much for me in the hospital. Confusion…upset…shock remained.

Ever so slightly, a minuscule amount of strength found its way to my extremities, and my limbs began to be able to move once again. They felt weighty and slow-moving—like I was on heavy medication or in recovery from surgery. But the exhaustion remained.

I remember Craig asking what I wanted to do. I remember not wanting to or being able to decide. My brain had ceased to be able to think coherently. The decision was made not to go to the hospital, and as the ambulance officers left, the hope of help seemed to depart with them.

Inside, my questions mounted, *How could they leave me here like this? What was going to happen?*

Soon after, we headed home as if nothing had happened.

The only thing was something HAD happened and was indeed happening.

My body had never felt such fatigue before. It was as if I'd been hit by a Mack truck or run a 100km marathon in a moment. Every part of me ached and screamed, "I'm so weary."

> A NEW SEED OF AFFLICTION AND FEAR THAT HAD BEEN PLANTED THAT NIGHT WOULD ENDEAVOR TO WREAK HAVOC IN OUR LIVES FOR MANY MONTHS AND YEARS TO COME.

I remained silent. No one spoke on the way home. The fear was palpable, and no one knew what to say. Ours was the quietest car trip our family had ever had.

The sounds of the tires on the road hurt my head; the glare of the streetlights stung my eyes. Sitting upright was a challenge as my head felt like a bowling ball. As we rattled along, my head leaned against the cold passenger window. Every bump, every knock, every turn felt and intensified. This was the longest car trip I'd ever had.

I plopped into bed, desperate for sleep. My eyelids closed as a signal for sleep to come, but it evaded me much of that night.

Fearful thoughts raced around and persisted for hours as the shock and trauma of what had occurred replayed inside my head. A new seed of affliction and fear that had been planted that night would endeavor to wreak havoc in our lives for many months and years to come.

The next morning, I woke, meaning I must've slept, but I felt no benefit, no refreshment or energy. My eyelids were heavy; my brain matter felt as if it was crystallizing inside like crackling ice as the temperature warms. So too was my head and its sensitivity to everything. The whole-body weakness persisted, and I struggled to stand, to talk, or to walk upright.

A barrage of thoughts tried to rattle my weary frame. *You have a brain tumor. You're going to die a slow, painful death. Your family will see it and be powerless. It'll be painful for them too. It's going to get worse*, and many more.

I was in the space of sheer terror; my pupils dilated almost wholly, and my snowlike complexion showed that things were not as they should be. Something was desperately wrong, and I was without solutions.

I felt a small and insignificant voice in a body that refused to obey my commands anymore.

I don't remember thinking of or speaking to God much during this time; I allowed fear to reign mostly in this space.

All I could squeak out in a moment of reprieve was a single word…"Help!"

He heard my cry, and help came.

Chapter One

REST

— Father's Heart —

My rest is an inner peace that remains whatever may come.

My rest refreshes the inner man so that the outer man can walk fearlessly forward into the plans I have for them.

My rest is the meeting place between you and Me.

It is where My Spirit speaks, and you hear Me.

*It is a perfect place of communion:
you and I walking together as we were designed to.*

My rest can be taken up or put down.

Walking in My rest is a choice.

*I will never force My rest upon you, child, because
My will is for you to choose Me—out of love.*

*In My rest, the cares and worries of the world do not
burden you as heavily because I give you the resources
of heaven and kingdom perspective.*

*In that place you and I accomplish unimaginable
things while we simply be with one another.*

Stop for a moment, child.

I call you child because no matter how old you may feel, compared to Me, you are always young, full of life, full of purpose, and full of My hope.

Pick up My peace and regain My rest.

Now walk forward in it.

If you find yourself overwhelmed or in fear, stop once more and take up My rest once again.

Are you weary, tired, burnt out?

Do you struggle to stop and be still?

I am.

I am here.

I am here for you, and I have wonderful truths to pour upon you in your wilting state.

Take heart; you will stand tall once again.

What you walk now is not the end but the beginning of something even more beautiful than before.

Come; let's walk a while, and I will bring you rest.

REST

— Take Aways —

In the storms where the enemy looks to steal my peace, in rest, God pours into me all that He knows I need, which helps to deflect the attacks and align me with heaven's heartbeat.

Rest is a reset button for my heart when overwhelmed by circumstances.

GOD'S REST DOESN'T DEMAND; IT INVITES.

Intimacy with God is sown and grown in rest.

Rest gives me permission to simply BE before Him.

Rest prioritizes my *being* over my *doing*.

God values me for who I am more than my doing or ability.

Rest is not only a position of the body but a state of the mind and heart.

Each time I choose to step into rest, draws me nearer to God.

REST CAN TRAVEL WITH ME WHEREVER I GO.

When I know what rest is and isn't for my design, I will recognize its absence. I can then choose to step back into it.

REST

Stepping into God's rest is a gradual wrestling of former ways being exchanged for the rhythms of His heart and His life-affirming and freeing ways.

GOD IS AT THE CENTER OF REST.

Discerning whether I am in or outside of rest often connects with how internally peaceful I am.

When I find myself outside of rest, I can become aware of God's presence, and rest soon follows.

Rest reflects the tender arms of the Father embracing His beloved child. Safe, gentle, comforting and healing.

I *get to* adopt God's view over what I am being governed by through a posture of rest. I can accept truth over lies, hope over hopelessness, and even life over death, which proves that rest might be advantageous for those of us walking through the harsh seasons.

— Questions to Ponder —

1. What words or phrases in the rest chapter leapt out to me?

2. What pace of life do I lead now? Does my pace align with my God wiring and design?

REST

3. What do I sense God is revealing to me about resting with Him?

> Come to me all who are weary and burdened, and I will give you rest. Take my yoke upon you and learn from me, for I am gentle and humble in heart, and you will find rest for your souls. For my yoke is easy, and my burden is light.
>
> **MATTHEW 11:28-30 NIV**

4. Are there any roadblocks to my being able to rest? What is God saying about them?

5. How do I envision Jesus resting? What does His rest look or feel like? What do I notice about how Jesus rests?

REST

6. What does my resting look and feel like for me? Am I content with my practice of resting with God? Why or why not? (refer to appendix 1 on page 335 for examples)

> And He said, "My Presence will go with you, and I will give you rest."
>
> **EXODUS 33:14 NKJV**

7. Are there any aspects of rest I desire?

8. What advantages could learning the art of rest bring to my current situation?

> Then Jesus said, "Let's go off by ourselves to a quiet place and rest awhile." He said this because there were so many people coming and going that Jesus and his apostles didn't even have time to eat.
>
> **MARK 6:31 NLT**

REST

9. How could I step towards God and the rest He has for me?

"I stand silently to listen for the one I love,
waiting as long as it takes for the Lord to rescue me.
For God alone has become my Savior.

He alone is my safe place;
his wraparound presence always protects me.
For he is my champion defender;
there's no risk of failure with God.

So why would I let worry paralyze me,
even when troubles multiply around me?"

PSALM 62:1-2 TPT

REST

— Rest Playlist —

You're Gonna Be Okay – Brian & Jenn Johnson

Breathe – Paul McClure

Secret Place – Phil Wickham

Psalm 42 – Tori Kelly

It Is Well with My Soul (hymn) – Horatio Spafford

Everyone Needs a Little – Kari Jobe

Just Be – Kim Walker-Smith

Unravelling – Cory Asbury

You Can Just Rest – Jenn Johnson & Hunter Thompson (Bethel Music)

Some restful instrumental tracks – Google "Worship music rest"

— Activations —

MUSICAL

Spend some time soaking in worship music.
Find something which has relaxing, restful tones.

Ask God to meet you in this time together.

VISUAL

Create a visual piece that reflects rest for you. As you
begin, ask God to meet you as you create.

When you are aware of an abiding peace or rest state, begin to create.
Spend some time thanking God for this.
Let His rest flow out into your artwork.

LOGICAL

Research Bible passages that mention or
reflect the practice of rest. List them as you find them.
Categorize and sort these, looking for patterns and observations.
In your personal study, ask God to reveal some
strategies and truths for you about rest.

REST

KINESTHETIC/BODILY

Close your eyes and become aware of your breathing. As your body and mind are stilled before the Lord, let Him bring You His peace…His rest… as you are simply before Him. Lay aside the busyness for the moment. Physically use your arms to symbolically lay down all else before Him.

Let this be a place where you only pick up what God is giving you.

INTRAPERSONAL

Sit with God in a quiet space and begin reflecting with Him about rest. How do you rest now?

What impacts your ability to rest? Consider how rest can be increased organically in your life.

VERBAL

Write a list of ways you know you are not in a state of rest.

List the ways you experience and recognize rest. (See Appendix 1 for some ideas.)

INTERPERSONAL

Talk with God or another trusted friend about rest. What does it mean to rest? What does biblical rest look and feel like? Consider keeping one another accountable in prioritizing rest in your week ahead.

NATURALISTIC

Consider God's creation and how it reflects the practice of rest. What evidence of rest can you find in nature? How can this be applied to your own life?

— Bless You —

I bless you, treasured one, with rest from any weariness.

Be blessed as you learn to momentarily step out of the chaos to simply be before Him.

Bless you in learning the easy yoke and light burden of the Lord.

I bless you with His peace.

His stillness.

His quietening.

I bless you with the knowledge and understanding that you are worthy, loved, and cherished by the Creator of the universe, who Himself gave you permission to step into rest, by modelling His rest to you.

Be blessed with the ability to stop for a moment.

To breathe and take in all that He has for you.

Bless you…with an ever-expanding awareness of His presence, and the rest, which is naturally found within it.

Bless you…with the ability to draw near to Him just as He draws near to you.

I bless you with the strength to lean into Father's rest—that place where He pours into you all that you need at this moment in time. Not coming in your own capacity, but His.

Bless you…with learning to draw from His abundant stores.

REST

I bless you with God's revelation that you can grow in rest with Him, which brings increased capacity and peace.

I pray that embracing His rest brings a wellspring of life to your journey with Him.

In Jesus' rest-filled name,

Amen.

XXXXX

Chapter Two

BE STILL

— Father's Heart —

Rush, rush, rush is what I see. Are you tired, beloved? Are you weary? Do you find yourself desiring rest but don't have a moment to yourself?

Come to Me. Come to Me, and I will give you rest (Matthew 11:28).

Stop focusing on doing and just be—before Me. When you are with others, it can often be like you are on a treadmill—always moving, talking, doing, or thinking about what you have to do— barely stopping. Simply being present in the moment is rare.

When you are with Me, just stop; be still.

Let your body rest before Me.

Let your mind rest for a bit.

Stop yourself from focusing on doing and just be—before Me. Take some deep breaths and drink in My rest for you. You might need to fight the tendency to talk or think or do. With Me, you don't need to do anything at this moment.

Initially, it may not be easy to step into being still.

Often your day is so busy that your body and mind are working overtime. So many tasks to complete and people to care for. Let Me reassure you, My child, there will always be an endless list of tasks and people who have needs.

*This moment right now will never be again. Let's enjoy
a moment together in the practice of being still.*

In My presence you can be refreshed and renewed.

*"Be still" is the place to pick up My peace. You can then go
out and have a clear perspective, make wise decisions, and
travel with Me through the day, feeling lighter.*

*When you come to be still with Me, you are allowing Me
to talk to you. Within the still, it will not be overwhelming
or busy, but a rewarding time of filling.*

Be still and just listen to whatever My Spirit reveals.

*The still will sometimes be tangible thoughts and answers, but often
it is merely about a Spirit-to-spirit time of just being. Soaking in
more of who I am reveals a greater measure of Myself in you.*

My presence is full of peace for your battle-worn emotions.

*My presence is love and acceptance when all around you cries out for
more. My presence is joy when all around you seek to bring you down.*

*Doesn't being in My presence sound refreshing to you? Come;
come to me, child, and be still before me. Offer Me a sacrifice of
time, and I will make it the best investment of your day. Your life
requires daily refreshment, and I am the answer to that need.*

*Come now, tell Me of your worries, your dreams, and your cares.
Then stop, be still, rest, and listen. Trust Me to bring all that you
need for the day ahead. Trust Me because I love you. My beloved, it
brings Me great joy when you choose to come and be still.*

BE STILL

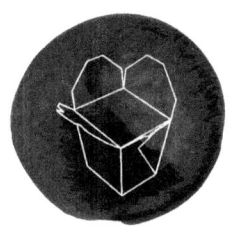

— *Take Aways* —

As I let go of my expectations and willingly embrace His words of life through being still before Him, it's then that I find hope winding its way back to the forefront of my heart and mind.

Be still is a space of abiding in God's presence.

IT'S A MOMENT,
A PRACTICE,
A STROLL
WITH HIM.

Be still can be a physical action or a place of abiding.

Being still is enough of an action when hardship hits.

Being still brings air to my lungs and peace to my inner world—whatever comes.

It doesn't demand answers but comes open-armed, willing to embrace all that God gives.

IN THE "BE STILL" I HEAR GOD FOR MYSELF (AND OTHERS).

My internal world can impact the outer state of being overwhelmed or changing the atmosphere His "Be still."

The more I encounter God's peace, the more I can confidently step into it when needed.

BE STILL

Being still is where I stop for a moment, exchanging the distractions and things that take from me—to pick up His peace.

GOD'S "BE STILL" CAN BE PICKED UP AT ANY MOMENT.

Being still doesn't require more of me; rather, it invests, gives, and pours into me. Be still is rest.

Being still is a choice to prioritize God above all else.

"Be still" is where I process my mess with Him, and He shows me how He is right there with me in it.

Being still is Spirit-to-spirit time, requiring nothing more than being open to what God wants to say or bring.

— Questions to Ponder —

1. How easily do I find being still? How do I cope when I have no other option than stillness?

   _____
   _____
   _____
   _____
   _____
   _____
   _____
   _____
   _____
   _____

2. What aspects of my life steal my ability to "Be still"? What elements help me enter into being still?

   _____
   _____
   _____

BE STILL

3. What words or phrases stood out to me as I read about being still with God?

> Be still and know that I am God; I will be exalted among the nations; I will be exalted in the earth.
>
> **PSALM 46:10 NIV**

CHAPTER TWO

4. What is God's truth about being still with Him?

5. Take note of what being still with God feels like. What do I sense? What do I observe about being in this kind of quiet? What is absent when I choose to abide in His stillness?

> Be still in the presence of the Lord, and wait patiently for him to act. Don't worry about evil people who prosper or fret about their wicked schemes.
>
> **PSALM 37:7 NLT**

6. Would this hardship be worth the journey if I flourished spiritually?

7. What riches have come because of this time? What part has my relationship with God played in gleaning these treasures?

> But they that wait upon the Lord shall renew their strength; they shall mount up with wings as eagles; they shall run, and not be weary; and they shall walk, and not faint.
>
> **ISAIAH 40:31 KJV**

CHAPTER TWO

8. How do I respond to this quote: "Being still with Him is what He desires for us, and yet it's often the last thing we engage in."

9. What advantages are there for my current circumstances if I chose to develop the art of "being still" and abiding in Him?

The LORD will fight for you;

you need only to be still.

EXODUS 14:14 NIV

BE STILL

— Be Still Playlist —

Be Still – Kari Jobe

Still – Rend Collective

Be Still – Red Rocks Worship

Our Breath Back (Spontaneous Worship) – Amanda Cook (Bethel Music)

Be Still – Hillsong

Oh, Come to the Altar – Elevation Worship

Peace – Bethel Music

Peace Be Still (featuring Lauren Daigle) – The Belonging Co.

Take Courage – Kristene DiMarco (Bethel Music)

— Activations —

MUSICAL

Ask God to expand His peace within you. Foster an awareness of "Be still" before Him while soaking in musical pieces. Check out the playlist and spend some time bringing Him a gift of worship.

VISUAL

Spend some time being still before God. Ask Him to give you words to describe stillness with Him.

Write, draw, create something which reflects what He reveals in this special time together.

LOGICAL

Consider what might prevent you from abiding in God's peace throughout life. How can this problem be resolved? Spend some time asking God for strategies which will help connect with His "Be still."

KINESTHETIC/BODILY

Find a relaxed position and space. Ask God to bring His stillness to each part of your body. Become aware of the individual parts to which He brings peace. Sense the growing expansion of His stillness. Enjoy and thank Him for all that He brings.

BE STILL

INTRAPERSONAL

Consider God's intention in instructing you to "Be still." How might this impact your current space?

How can you best step into God's stillness when rougher waters stir? What do you notice internally when you step into "Be still"?

VERBAL

Take a moment to find verses about 'Be Still.' Declaring aloud declaring aloud what God says in His Word about, "Be Still." Allow each verse some stillness following its declaration. Let God's Word invest, allowing its truth to land within you. Give Him specific thankfulness for the investment.

INTERPERSONAL

Ponder how you stepping into God's stillness might impact those around you. Discuss these ideas with a trusted friend. Spend some time praying together. Thoroughly enjoying God's stillness together.

NATURALISTIC

Find a peaceful space outside. Sit, stand, whatever feels most relaxing. Ask God to still your inner world. Become aware of enjoying and adopting His stillness. Take note of the wind and its impact upon the leaves. Like the wind, become aware of going where God leads with His breeze.

— Bless You —

I bless you, precious reader, with permission to take a few minutes to "Be still" before God.

I bless you with an awareness of God's presence and the peace that comes with it.

I bless you with regular encounters of "Be still."

Be blessed with times where you commune with God's heart. Where He pours into you all that He knows you need in that moment.

Let being still foster an increasing intimacy between the two of you.

I bless you with an awareness of the absence of stillness. When circumstances are looking to overtake you, be blessed with the ability to stop in these times and "be still" in your body, mind, and heart.

Bless you… with being able to pick up His peace— that posture of "Be still" at any moment.

I bless you with Father's rhythm and pace for life.

Bless you… with the ability to wait upon the Lord, so that your strength will be renewed.

I bless you with the experience of knowing the love of the Father through this time of "Be still."

I bless you with the ability to step into God's "Be still" at any moment and have all the clutter or noise fade away.

Be blessed with the knowledge that as you are still, the Lord fights on your behalf.

Bless you…with tangible encounters with the presence of God as you choose to still yourself before Him.

In Jesus' peaceful name,

Amen.

xxxxx

Chapter Three

GIVING AND RECEIVING

— Father's Heart —

"Oh, My precious child, let Me lavish My love upon you during this time.

I have abundant supplies readily available for you.

*I have told you to ask anything in My name, and
you will receive that your joy may be full.*

Do you believe this, My child?

Will you choose to trust Me?

I know that at times you've felt guilty about receiving from others.

These ones I send bring you symbols of My love, My attention, and care.

*You are so special to Me; I have not forgotten you
and have much in store for you, My love.*

Just as you have poured into others, I desire to pour into you.

Take heart, when you receive from ones such as these, You receive from Me.

When you welcome them in, you welcome Me in.

*As you feel the warmth that comes from being seen
and cared for in these ways, you accept Me.*

You are My precious child; I want to nurture you if you will allow Me.

Understand that I've made you to give and to receive in life. Not one wholly or the other. But seasons, moments of giving and receiving.

Receiving in My kingdom is also to give.

To give to others is also to receive.

To give and receive from a pure heart—well, there is no greater gift.

I am the true giver and the One you will receive from constantly. My desire is to be abundantly generous to My children.

This is lived out in relationship with Me.

But by receiving from others, you also receive from Me.

There is much in your life vying for your energy and time.

Where will you choose to invest it? Will you come alongside Me and commune?

I have kingdom adventures for you and me to unite in. Never before will you experience such blessing than when you have chosen to partner with the plans of My heart.

My heart and yours in sweet embrace.

My provision poured out, My words, My acts of love…I have brought these and more for you to be a part of, My beloved.

I invite you each day.

Come, let's adventure together, let's talk and walk a while, and I will lift you to higher plains of giving and receiving."

GIVING AND RECEIVING

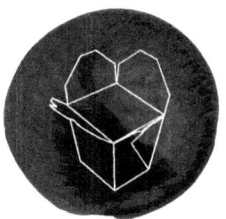

— *Take Aways* —

Anything I receive from another person in this tough season is a gift from God—a special love note from Him. I must let go of my pride and accept His gift with thanks. Then praise God for thinking of me enough to send the gift.

Being an island in life makes it harder for me to receive.

Learning how to receive is important to God.

SOMETIMES I NEED TO ASK FOR WHAT I NEED.

Receiving can be a humbling but a character-honing experience.

Intimacy with God is increased as I learn to receive well from Him.

> He sees all, knows all, and cares about all. My needs are not unseen.

> I receive refreshment just as I have brought refreshment to others.

> Givers aren't just giving; they are also being blessed as I receive.

> Making my need known takes strength—both to God and others as prompted.

> If I only ever give, how can I learn how to receive from Him?

> Things work well as I share what I have with those who need it.

SOME SEASONS, IT'S ME WHO RECEIVES THESE LIFELINES.

> There are giving seasons and seasons of receiving. When I am walking through tough, it might be my time to receive.

GIVING AND RECEIVING

I can give and receive in various ways. Acts of service, gifts, finances, prayer, time, physical touch, encouragement, words of hope, the fruit of the Spirit, encounters with God, practical needs.

I was born to connect with others in giving and receiving.

As I give, God often gives me the fringe benefit of receiving in the process.

To reject another's offer of help is to sometimes turn away away from God's gift to me in my time of need.

God is the ultimate gift giver, Jesus.

IT IS A BLESSING TO GIVE AND TO RECEIVE.

It feels good to give—even if it costs.

He prompts me at the exact moment another village person is failing; therefore, I do what He prompts. It lifts them for another day, spurring them on to keep going until something shifts.

— Questions to Ponder —

1. What do I believe about giving and receiving? How were giving and receiving modelled to me in my family?

2. How easy is it for me to ask for help when I need it? Why or why not? What are the influencing factors?

GIVING AND RECEIVING

3. What has been my response when others have blessed me during a time of challenge?

> "Until now, you have asked nothing in My name. Ask, and you will receive, that your joy may be full."
>
> **JOHN 16:24 NKJV**

4. What has been my experience with both giving and receiving? Are there specific memories of good or poor experiences?

5. Am I willing to have a season of receiving? What if through it I learnt to give even better than before? Would this change my willingness to receive?

> Yes, God is more than ready to overwhelm you with every form of grace so that you will have more than enough of everything — every moment and in every way. He will make you overflow with abundance in every good thing you do.
>
> **2 CORINTHIANS 9:8 TPT**

GIVING AND RECEIVING

6. Is it possible that God is teaching me to learn how to receive well from Him through this experience? Would knowing this make it easier for me to receive?

7. What biblical examples can I find about giving and receiving? What does Jesus say about it?

> All generous giving and every perfect gift is from above, coming down from the Father of lights, with whom there is no variation or the slightest hint of change.
>
> **JAMES 1:17 NET**

8. Am I willing to allow others to help me? How comfortable am I with receiving? Why or why not?

9. When I consider my giving and receiving, which do I feel more comfortable doing? What does God say about my practices of both?

> Give, and it will be given to you: good measure, pressed down, shaken together, and running over, will be given to you. For with the same measure you measure, it will be measured back to you.
>
> **LUKE 6:38 WEB**

10. What advantages might practising these with God bring to my life and the lives of others? What might this bring to hard seasons and my experience of them?

The Lord is trustworthy in all he promises
and faithful in all he does.
The Lord upholds all who fall
and lifts up all who are bowed down.
The eyes of all look to you,
and you give them their food at the proper time.
You open your hand
and satisfy the desires of every living thing.
The Lord is righteous in all his ways
and faithful in all he does.
The Lord is near to all who call on him,
to all who call on him in truth.

PSALM 145:13B-18 NIV

GIVING AND RECEIVING

— Giving and Receiving Playlist —

Indescribable – Chris Tomlin

No Longer Slaves – Jonathan David Helser (Bethel Music)

You're Not Alone – Marie Miller

You Are Beloved – Jordan Feliz

Goodness of God – Jenn Johnson

Less Like Me – Zach Williams

— Activations —

MUSICAL

Go on an exploration song journey, discovering some fresh worship music, which reflect either receiving from God or giving to God. Pour out your heart to Him in this time.

VISUAL

Create a gift for God. Try to capture how your heart feels towards Him and His gifts to you. Think upon this phrase: "God loved me first— before I could bring Him anything."

LOGICAL

Make a list of moments of receiving you've encountered during this time of trial. Consider the benefits of learning to both give and receive well. What are the spiritual/physical/emotional/ psychological benefits?

KINESTHETIC/BODILY

Kick your shoes off and walk in the grass. Enjoy the crinkle of each blade beneath your feet. As you do this, ponder the moments where God has given. How did you respond to these gifts? Ask Him what He wants to tell you in this time about receiving or giving.

GIVING AND RECEIVING

INTRAPERSONAL

Ponder giving and receiving with God. Ask Him some key questions. E.g. "What is my heart motivation for giving and receiving? Is it for them, myself or both? Are there any lies I believe about giving or receiving?" Ask God for His truth. How can learning to receive better impact your intimacy with God?

VERBAL

Write God a love letter, thanking Him for who or what He has given to you in this time. Name them.

Bless them. Thank Him for these provisions.

INTERPERSONAL

Discuss with a trusted friend, biblical examples of when giving and receiving were modelled well. Consider some special times where you've experienced the thrill of a need met. Pray with one another, asking God to reveal whether He wants you to give or receive in this time.

NATURALISTIC

Observe how giving and receiving are an integral part of creation's design. How are they reflected in nature? What is God revealing about giving and receiving through these visual examples?

CHAPTER THREE

— Bless You —

Be blessed one who God loves first.

I bless you with clarity about your own ability to give and receive.

Be blessed with permission to receive well.

Bless you… with increase in receiving from others, especially God.

Be blessed in the ways you give and receive.

I bless you with permission to learn how to receive His good gifts.

I bless you with understanding, "when I know how to receive well, I also know how to give well."

Be blessed with fresh revelation: "as I have poured into others, so I will be poured into."

I bless you with refreshment as you receive.

Bless you… as you experience the beautiful rhythm of giving and receiving well.

Bless you… with aha moments of revelation with God. In sharing what you have with others and receiving from others in this season.

As Jesus brings encounters with His HUGE heart of love for you, be blessed through receiving.

In Jesus' generous, faithful and loving name,

Amen.

xxxxx

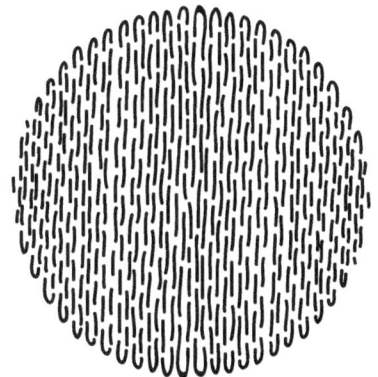

Chapter Four

ATMOSPHERE

— Father's Heart —

"I am the King of all environments. No atmosphere or situation is greater than I am.

As I live in you, you take My presence wherever you go. As you become more conscious of our journeying together, I will equip you with everything you need.

When an atmosphere is heavy and burdening, bring Me into your situation, and there will be shift.

Acknowledge and trust Me wherever you find yourself.

I am tangible and real. Although you don't often see My form with your eyes, I am more real than anything you might see.

The spirit realm is continually moving, as do I.

I never sleep. As you become aware of Me, you will experience what happens when I come into a situation. The weight of heaviness is shared between us both.

I love nothing better than to carry the bulk. Bringing redemptive elements for you in what remains.

Cast your heaviness on Me. My Son died so you don't have to live under burdens anymore.

Flow with My Spirit. He will lift the air around you just because you are there, and He lives within it and within you.

Oppressive atmospheres, negativity, or lack? These are My kinds of spaces, which I love to infiltrate and redeem through you.

What can stand against you as I dwell in you? Nothing.

Do you have opposition, fear, upset, anxiety, or grief?

Let Me shift that for you. Let Me exchange the atmosphere for My truth.

Let Me inject My peace, My love, My comfort, My embrace into your situation.

I do not do this so that you might be comfortable, but that we would commune with one another. And that you might share with others the reason for your joy and hope.

That you would be a temple for My Holy Spirit, and that temple is brought into the world to change the world.

In Me, you are a true world changer.

Start small if you are unsure; I don't mind small beginnings.

Those small steps of trust lead to greater confidence in My ability to work-whatever comes your way.

Nothing stands in the way of My ability to change atmospheres and circumstances."

ATMOSPHERE

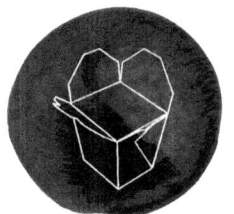

— Take Aways —

Holy Spirit is 100 percent complete, and lives inside of me. Therefore, wherever I am, He is also there. He brings with Him the power to bless any atmosphere at any time.

What I fill my mind and heart with can have physical, emotional, mental, and spiritual ramifications atmospherically and in certain circumstances.

God and the enemy both influence atmospheres— one for the good, the other for the oppressive.

The things of God's nature positively affect my atmosphere; the opposite is also true.

EVERY ATMOSPHERE CAN BE LIFTED/ SHIFTED/ IMPACTED BY THE POWERFUL, LIFE-GIVING PRESENCE OF THE FATHER.

CHAPTER FOUR

- My health can be impacted by the spiritual atmosphere of my home and other environments.

- I can inadvertently open doors which aren't healthy for me.

- Various atmospheres can impact my life, including physically, spiritually, emotionally, mentally—heartwise and thoughtwise.

- Asking God to reveal and assess the health of the atmospheres which impact me brings me closer to healthier atmospheres and His blessing.

I AM NOT A PRISONER OF MY ATMOSPHERE WHEN I WALK WITH GOD.

- God is ready, willing, and able to create an atmosphere with me that is peaceful.

- Becoming more aware of God than anything around or in me, is the first step to instigating a spiritual atmospheric shift.

ATMOSPHERE

When I focus only on my circumstances, I find I am filled with thoughts outside of God that include fear, anxiety, worry, and negative focus. These contrary emotions add nothing good to my life—only generate more of the same.

THE ATMOSPHERE AROUND ME CAN BLESS, ENCOURAGE, COMFORT, AND HEAL.

Holy Spirit can cleanse defiled spaces. He loves to redeem them!

Having healthy lines of communication with God means there's nothing for me to fear.

With God, there is hope for redemption of any atmosphere.

Not all things are good. Some items may negatively impact the atmosphere. Asking Holy Spirit to reveal these and instructions as to what to do with them is healthy for my atmosphere and me.

— *Questions to Ponder* —

1. Was there something specific about atmospheres that jumped out for me?

2. What do I notice about atmospheres and their impact on my peace levels?

ATMOSPHERE

3. What do I believe about my current environment and the atmosphere and its impact upon me?

> By faith, we understand that the entire universe was formed at God's command, that what we now see did not come from anything that can be seen.
>
> **HEBREWS 11:3 NLT**

4. Has there ever been a time where meeting someone or walking into a space brought a dark feeling? How about incredible peace or a joyful atmosphere? What do I believe is happening in these times?

5. Am I aware of a time where God has shifted an atmosphere for me? What did He do? What did He bring? How was it different?

Let them construct a sanctuary for Me, that I may dwell among them.

EXODUS 25:8 NASB

ATMOSPHERE

6. Is there an atmosphere or aspect of the atmosphere that I need shifted today?

7. Ask God to highlight if there is anything which is influencing the environment around me or bringing negative feelings to my home. Then ask Him what to do with it.

> The spiritual did not come first, but the natural, and after that, the spirit.
>
> 1 CORINTHIANS 15:46 NIV

8. Thinking about my home environment, do I have a space that is life-giving to me? Can I create one? What would this feel like? What advantages might this bring to my circumstance?

9. What kind of environment is life-giving for me?

> And He said, "My Presence will go with you, and I will give you rest."
>
> **EXODUS 33:14 NKJV**

ATMOSPHERE

6. Is there an atmosphere or aspect of the atmosphere that I need shifted today?

7. Ask God to highlight if there is anything which is influencing the environment around me or bringing negative feelings to my home. Then ask Him what to do with it.

> The spiritual did not come first, but the natural, and after that, the spirit.
>
> **1 CORINTHIANS 15:46 NIV**

8. Thinking about my home environment, do I have a space that is life-giving to me? Can I create one? What would this feel like? What advantages might this bring to my circumstance?

9. What kind of environment is life-giving for me?

> And He said, "My Presence will go with you, and I will give you rest."
>
> **EXODUS 33:14 NKJV**

ATMOSPHERE

10. Have I ever considered that even in this hardship, God may partner with me to change an atmosphere for someone else?

For this is what the Lord says—
he who created the heavens, he is God,
He who fashioned and made the earth, he founded it;
He did not create it to be empty,
but formed it to be inhabited—he says;
"I am the Lord, and there is no other."

ISAIAH 45:18 NIV

ATMOSPHERE

— Atmosphere Playlist —

Chains Are Breaking – Planetshakers

Rooftops – Jesus Culture

I Wonder – Leeland

My Hands Are Open – Josh Baldwin (Bethel Music)

Torrential Love – Stairway Music

A Place Called Earth – Jon Foreman ft. Lauren Daigle

Stand in Your Love – Cory Asbury & Brandon Lake

Fly – Jason Upton

— Activations —

MUSICAL

Select an atmosphere which God has highlighted as needing some attention. Select some appropriate music which brings what God highlights to you. E.g. if He has highlighted a fearful atmosphere, play some peaceful, empowering worship of declaration of trust in Him. Check out the playlist or Samuel Barbers "Adagio for Strings" for an example of how music can influence atmosphere.

VISUAL

Physically create a space or room which reflects safety and peace—a place where connecting with God is made easier. Decorate, pray over and bless that area. Ask Holy Spirit to inspire your heart and give you ideas for this space.

LOGICAL

Assess the different atmospheres in and around you. Categorise which ones are healthy and life-giving. Ask God to highlight any areas He wants to tweak, redeem or lift.

KINESTHETIC/BODILY

Walk through your home, asking God to reveal an
area He wants to upgrade supernaturally.

Ask Him what part you can play in blessing the atmosphere of your home.

INTRAPERSONAL

Consider the environment around you, especially the atmosphere of
your heart and mind. Do certain aspects steal joy? Do people, places
or things seem to take more from you than you have to give?

Spend some time pondering the areas and atmospheres that
need some fresh, kingdom insight and investment.

VERBAL

In your journal, note the various atmospheres in your life. Spend some
time with God, asking Him for an atmosphere assessment and any
actions that would improve it. Write a declaration of blessing over your
home and any atmosphere that has been highlighted by Him.

INTERPERSONAL

Connect with a trusted mentor who has experience in praying over the
home. (Ask God to reveal someone if you don't yet know of someone
or ask Holy Spirit what to do, then do that.) Then walk through your
home with them, anoint it with oil and bless it in Jesus' name.

NATURALISTIC

Consider a plant which is tended to, fed and provided with
all that it needs. Compare this to one that has been neglected.
Consider how this applies to the atmospheres in your life.

— Bless You —

*I bless you with an atmosphere that adds health
to your body and healing to your bones.*

I bless you with an environment that speaks life to your mind, heart and body.

I bless you with the ability to see God's view of your home and all atmospheres.

I bless you with clarity about your atmosphere.

*Bless you… with a home environment that is pure and holy,
bringing life and health to all who live or visit there.*

I bless you with an atmosphere of restoration and rest.

May the atmosphere of your heart, mind, body and home be blessed with joy.

Bless you… with attuned senses to the kingdom elements of any atmosphere.

*I bless you with the ability to hear what God wants to say
about your possessions and home. Be blessed with courage and
obedience to trust and follow what God reveals to you.*

*Be blessed with an atmosphere where Holy Spirit loves to dwell, bringing
His presence with Him, which will revive the lowly and lift the heart.*

*I bless you with light, with warmth, with encountering His heart today
and all days in Jesus' powerfully peaceful and redemptive name.*

Amen.

xxxxx

Chapter Five

NEVER ALONE

— Father's Heart —

"How can I communicate to you more strongly about how much I love you?

I tell you that you are never alone, yet you don't always feel it, you don't always see it, and doubt can creep in.

Trust Me, My precious child.

I created you before the beginning of time. My mind knew the inner workings of your entire being. I knew how you would live, what your personality would be. I even knew the special moments we would share throughout your lifetime here on earth.

All of this, well before you were born.

I have created you from dust, someone so entirely precious to Me from something that seems relatively worthless.

If you understood the value I place upon you, you would never question whether or not you were alone. That you are alone is simply a lie.

My truth is that you are very much known, and I am your constant companion.

I love you, My child.

You are remembered every second of the day and night. I love you, My child.

You have no idea how many thoughts I have about you. They outnumber the grains of sand on all the beaches of the world.

You are so special to Me.

You hold such great worth and importance to Me.

I know there have been times when you felt worthless and unimportant; that too is a lie.

I exist, and I cover everything. My Spirit moves over the earth, and My heavenly beings and I watch over you.

I am fully aware of what you are feeling right at this moment…and I care.

I am not absent or far away, as you sometimes feel, but I am closer than your breath. I love you that much.

My beloved, when you feel isolated, come to Me.

Decide to wait with Me and upon Me.

Ask Me to reveal Myself to you, and I will fill the empty space.

I will do this because it is who I am, and it is what I LOVE to do—especially for you."

NEVER ALONE

— Take Aways —

Some seasons are designed to be traveled alone in order to connect with God. Connecting with God grows intimacy between us—if I allow it to.

God allows me to see how much He is in everything. This truth reassures me that I am not alone.

WHEN I DON'T KNOW THE NEXT STEP, GOD DOES.

Despite how I feel, I am never alone because God is WITH me. He is my constant.

God is the only One who knows, understands, cares about and can meet my need 100 percent.

I will come out of this season stronger for having chosen to walk with God in it.

Seasons of human isolation draw me closer to the One who, time and time again, proves that He is my perfect friend.

Intimacy with God can be wholly satisfying—when I feel alone.

Coming to peace about walking through tough times with God releases the pressure on others to be my answer.

GOD IS CLOSE TO THOSE WHO ARE BROKEN; THIS IS HIS PERSONAL PROMISE TO ME.

Seasons of dependence upon God can reframe, reboot relational, physical, emotional, mental and spiritual health and intimacy.

NEVER ALONE

As I choose to put my hand in His for all my needs—even in the waiting, He provides the things I didn't even know I needed—but satisfy my heart.

IN THIS TIME, MY KINGDOM IDENTITY IS BEING REVEALED.

When I place God above all others in my life, this brings a different experience of my circumstances—than when I place others before Him.

People can let me down at times, but God is steadfast and trustworthy.

My precious friends and family cannot be with me 24/7. However, God is! He promises this to me.

Don't entertain guilt or shame for not turning to God before now. Start now—in the present moment and walk forward hand in hand with Him.

— *Questions to Ponder* —

1. Have there been times in this season when I have felt alone? What has contributed to this feeling?

2. Thinking back upon these times, what has helped? How had God played a part in this?

3. What aspects of this chapter leaped out? What keywords or phrases? What is God showing me about myself?

> No one will be able to stand up against you, all the days of your life; As I was with Moses, so I will be with you; I will never leave you nor forsake you.
>
> **JOSHUA 1:5 NIV**

4. The next time I feel alone, what is my plan of action? Does this strategy align with God's plan of action for me? Ask Him some questions about my intentions.

5. Ask God whether there are any lies I believe about this season and being alone? Have I asked God what the truth is? Thank Him for this truth as He reveals it to me.

> Be sure of this: I am with you always, even to the end of the age.
>
> **MATTHEW 28:20B NLT**

6. What is the truth that I can tell myself when I feel alone?

7. What are the benefits of walking forward in the truth that God is always with me?

> The one who sent me is with me; he has not left me alone, for I always do what pleases Him.
>
> **ROMANS 8:38-39 NLT**

8. Is there anything that I sense that God wants me to do or believe differently because of this truth?

9. What does the Bible say about being alone? How do I know that these words are true? What action can I take to solidify these promises in my heart during the tough time?

> Don't be afraid, for I am with you. Don't be discouraged, for I am your God. I will strengthen you and help you. I will hold you up with my victorious right hand.
>
> **ISAIAH 41:10 NLT**

— Never Alone Playlist —

God I look to You – Jenn Johnson

Never Alone – Tori Kelly

He Knows My Name – Tommy Walker

Singing Over Me – Kari Jobe

It Is Well – Kristene DiMarco

Another in the Fire – Hillsong United

You Will Never Run – Rend Collective

I am not alone - Kari Jobe

Leave the 99 - Audio Adrenaline

CHAPTER FIVE

— *Activations* —

MUSICAL

Select a portion of Scripture about God's never leaving you, which is most meaningful to you personally. Express to God your thanks. Vocalise, make a joyful noise to Him in thanks for this truth. You are free to worship Him in this way. Go with His flow and attune to His leading.

VISUAL

Envision what God being with you looks and feels like. Express this mental image in a creative way. Ask God for a picture or an impression. Ask God for a special place where you can meet together with Him. Spend time in this place. How do you feel when you are there with Him? What is good about this place? What can you take from this experience into your day?

LOGICAL

Explore the word and this theme of "never alone." How many Scriptures in the Bible reassure you of this truth? What can you take away from this search? What aspects of God's nature does this personal study reveal to you?

KINESTHETIC/BODILY

Using only your body, create a visual representation of what "God and I United" looks and feels like.

Be released to use physical symbols as you thank Him, using your body for His constant presence.

INTRAPERSONAL

Think upon God's nature and how the truth of "He is always with me" is reflected in your life.

What is God's heart desire for you to embrace this truth? How would life be different if you adopted and walked out this truth in your everyday?

VERBAL

Spend some time reading the verses which speak about "never alone." Take each verse and personalise it, writing them as "I" statements and declarations of God's truth. E.g.: Based on Deuteronomy 31:6 (NIV), "I will be strong and courageous. I will not be afraid or terrified because the Lord my God goes with me. I will never be left or forgotten by Him.'

INTERPERSONAL

Consider the outcomes of walking forward in this truth and not walking in this truth. How might the outcome of choosing to adopt and walk in the truth of "He is always with me" impact your and others in life?

NATURALISTIC

What evidence in the natural world can you find of God's being constantly with you? How does He reveal Himself through creation? What reminders do you encounter each day that you are never alone?

CHAPTER FIVE

— Bless You —

*I bless you, precious reader, with the experience
of God's being with you at every turn.*

I bless you with His great, abiding peace at this time.

I bless you with eyes to see what He has already given you in this season.

*Bless you…with fearlessness and a greater
revelation of God's being with you always.*

Be blessed with a greater trust in Him in your most vulnerable moments.

*I bless you with this truth: "No one and nothing can stand
against you all the days of your life, because He is with you."*

Be blessed in your comings and your goings.

*God bless you, your family, your friends, your medical practitioners,
and those with whom you have yet to come into contact.*

*Bless you…with increase in knowing that nothing
can separate you from the love of God.*

*I bless you with an awareness that you have all you need
simply because God is with you wherever you are.*

*Be blessed with strength and courage to choose to
rise—even when you don't feel like it.*

*Be blessed with the experience that whenever you cry out to
Him, He answers you swiftly with His loving presence.*

*I bless you with a God revelation that He is with you
always and that you are never, ever alone.*

In Jesus' name,

Amen

xxxxx

Chapter Six

SAFE PLACES, SAFE PEOPLE

— Father's Heart —

*"I have placed My Holy Spirit within you. Part of His
ways are to show you the truth about all things.*

It is essential to know My heart for you is for your good.

*When you accept this truth, it becomes much easier to
discern the best way forward—with Me.*

I am your safe place.

*I have placed people around you who, like you, have needs and desires.
Some of those needs and desires are healthy, and others are not.*

*My heart is that my children would live together in love, encouraging, considering,
and serving one another. Giving grace and forgiveness where and when needed.*

*You are always safe with Me, beloved, but not all people and places are
safe all the time. My desire is that you would have connection with safe
people. Understand that no one person is wholly secure all the time. This
is because all people are on their own journey through life and growth.*

*As you place Me at the forefront, you will experience complete safety in
love. By encountering Me in this way, you will see aspects of Me in others.*

As you connect with others, you may experience disappointment or hurt.

*Take heart…with Me as your foundation, you will become
accustomed to what safe places and people look and feel like.*

Ask My Spirit for guidance as He won't lead you astray.

I will never bring fear or confusion. These things are not a part of My heart.

Know Me, and you will recognize what is or isn't My best for you.

Not all people have you in mind as they speak or act; they too are mid-process. Forgive, My child. Forgive and bless those who have brought anything other than life to you. If their words or actions are in direct opposition to My words, then release them; don't hold onto these things. They are burdens you don't need to carry.

You have permission to weigh up others' words with Me. Let Me reveal My truth to you, precious one.

Rest assured, I have designed you to have healthy boundaries. I only ask of you what I have resourced and prepared you for.

Saying yes to all things and all people is never the way forward. I want you to say yes to the things and people I discern for you.

Place your expectations and needs at My feet and watch how I bring the right people at the right times to you.

I know your heart longs to connect with healthy people and be in safe relationship. I have designed you for village life with others. Understand that the only wholly complete friendship is Mine. Once you welcome this truth, relationships with others will be healthier.

You have believed that to care for those in community, you must be self-sacrificing. I never asked you to be the sacrifice—only to bring others to the One who was the sacrifice for them.

Love others wholeheartedly as I lead you, give them grace in their own growth, and you will find they will leave more deposits than withdrawals.

Hold Me tightly and hold others lightly, beloved one.

You now know the way; follow it."

SAFE PLACES AND SAFE PEOPLE

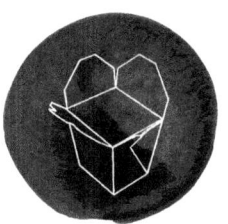

— *Take Aways* —

Be aware that each person I share with has his or her own filters, brokenness, and experiences. Not all will be able to understand or empathize with what I am going through.

God is the only 100-percent, genuinely safe place and person, BUT He encourages me to live in community.

Ask God to match my need with the right person at the right time.

SAFETY IS CONNECTED TO HAVING HEALTHY BOUNDARIES.

Through these reflections I see and appreciate aspects of many beautiful friends whom God has given me in my life.

Asking God who my safe people are for this season is always good.

Safe people are encouragers who speak life words and reflect the Father back to us in times of tough.

Safe places have been a vital piece of the puzzle for me. Disengaging with the places and people that take from my depleted tank helps me to simply "be" before God.

If I find myself in a situation where I am threatened, I close up, unable to give much of myself at all.

SAFE PLACES LEAVE ME BETTER FOR HAVING BEEN THERE EVERY TIME.

It benefits me and others to understand and articulate my need when I am able. If I am not able, asking God to articulate and meet it works as well.

All relationships are a risk, but if I never step out onto the rope, I will not experience the delight of walking in high places with true friends.

Safe people reflect aspects of God's heart back to me and I to them.

SAFE PLACES AND SAFE PEOPLE

In this life, I will be misunderstood and misunderstand others. I will need to forgive and to be forgiven. Ideally, I will give myself and others permission to make mistakes and grow from them.

SAFETY DEVELOPS DEPTH IN INTIMACY.

Safe people and places encourage me to be myself without shame or fear.

God keeps me safe as I take refuge in Him. Just as He showed Himself through Jesus and reflects Himself to me now through His Word.

Safety is strongly connected with my ability to be authentic and vulnerable with those around me.

When I live in safety, I blossom like a rose and feel safe to unfold, to bloom, to thrive, to release a sweet-smelling fragrance, and to display all my color in life. This, in turn, blesses and encourages others, which enables others to share in similar ways.

— *Questions to Ponder* —

1. Who are my safe people? Where are my safe places?

2. When have I experienced a safe place or person at precisely the right time? How did this impact me?

3. How does God view safety? What is He saying about this? Does the Bible have specific examples of this? (see appendix 3, page 347 for futher inspiration.)

Do to others as you would have them do to you.

LUKE 6:31 NIV

4. Are there people or places that aren't safe for me in this season? How am I managing this? How do I feel towards them? How do healthy boundaries relate to safety? What is God saying?

5. Am I a safe person for others? Why or why not? What evidence is there of this?

It is better to take refuge in the Lord than to trust in humans.

PSALM 118:8 NIV

6. What qualities do I need a safe person to have? Are there varying levels of safety? Are there different people for different purposes in my life?

7. Have I received some unhelpful judgment, words, or experiences which have made this season more difficult? What does God say about what was said and done?

> Whoever walks in integrity, walks securely, but whoever takes crooked paths will be found out.
>
> **PROVERBS 10:9 NIV**

8. Am I willing to travel less intimately with those who are not safe for me at this time? What is God saying about these relationships? As I think upon the idea of distancing myself, what happens to my personal peace levels?

9. Is there any way I can create a safe place with God in this season? What does this space look and feel like? What qualities will it exude?

Oil and perfume makes the heart glad, and the sweetness of a friend comes from his earnest counsel.

PROVERBS 27:9 ESV

10. If I find myself without safe people, am I willing to allow God to be my safe place at this time? Is He enough for me? Talk to Him about this.

11. What would it bring to my experience of hardship, knowing I had safe people with whom to journey? How would this help? What benefits would be having safe people and places available to me?

> You are my hiding place.
> You will protect me from
> trouble and surround me
> with songs of deliverance.
>
> **PSALM 32:7 NIV**

In peace, I will both lie down and sleep,
For You alone, O Lord, make me to dwell in safety.

PSALM 4:8 NIV

SAFE PLACES AND SAFE PEOPLE

— Safe Places, Safe People Playlist —

You Make Me Brave – Amanda Cooke

Healer – Kari Jobe

Keeper of My Heart – Kari Jobe

Your Wings – Lauren Daigle

No One Every Cared for Me Like Jesus – Steffany Gretzinger

The Worship Medley – Tauren Wells ft. Davies

Truth Be Told – Matthew West

— *Activations* —

MUSICAL

Spend some time giving thanks to God for His complete safety. Use voice or instrument to express your praise of Him. Give thanks for His provision of safe people and places for you in this season.

VISUAL

Visualise a set of traffic lights with God. Ask Him specifically about a relationship you currently are unsure about its safety. Ask Him to reveal, using the traffic lights whether this person is: Green=Safe. Amber=Wait/not right now, or share with caution. Red=Unsafe

LOGICAL

Looking at the life of Jesus, can you find specific examples of when He encountered safe and unsafe people? What qualities did they exude as people? What was His response to them? How might this help you in your current season?

KINESTHETIC/BODILY

Using your body, create something to represent the safety you experience with God. If you haven't as yet experienced this, ask God to give you an encounter of this or to highlight when you have been protected by Him. Give God thanks for the safe people and places He has provided at this time.

INTRAPERSONAL

Consider the times you've have been led down a road of hurt because you placed trust in an unsafe person/place. This kind of experience has the potential to teach you about the type of person you wish to become and be for others. What pieces of gold can you glean from that experience? How can it be applied to the area of safety? Ask God for His view on that experience.

VERBAL

Consider this quote: "I give myself permission to share my life with those who are trustworthy, mature, and loving. I don't have to share my full self with everyone all the time. Boundaries are an essential part of health for me in this season." Do you agree? Why or why not? How would you amend or add to this declaration to fit your situation?

INTERPERSONAL

Connect with a trusted friend over a coffee and chat about safety. The following are some conversation starters if you need them: What does a safe person look like? When have I experienced safety/danger?

What does a godly safe person look like? Study the life of Jesus together. How was Jesus for others and is now safe for you? See Appendix 3 for some reflections.

NATURALISTIC

Ponder the natural world and how safety is essential for health, life, and growth. What happens when safety is absent? How is protection an essential part of life in creation? How can these reflections be applied to this current season? What can you learn from what you see in God's creation?

— Bless You —

Be blessed, one who is worthy of safety,

Bless you… with the ability to see those who are safe around you.

Bless you… as you take refuge in the Lord first.

God bless you with healing from unsafe situations and people of the past.

Be blessed with people who are trustworthy, loving, and able to walk alongside of you in this challenging time.

Bless you… with protection, security, and companionship.

I bless you with health in relationships.

Bless you… with revelations about places that are safe for you.

Be blessed as you walk hand in hand with Jesus, your safe haven and protector.

In the fiercely protective and loving arms of Jesus,

Amen.

XXXXX

Chapter Seven

TRUST

— Father's Heart —

"I know much of what you have experienced in this world has made it difficult to trust at times.

I want you to know I was there with you the entire time.

I was holding your hand, weeping with you, protecting and tending to you, all the while knowing if you chose to allow Me, I would carry it for you.

I would not only carry the burden but deal with it on your behalf, tossing it to the farthest part of the universe, never to plague you again.

Trusting Me is closely connected to having hope.

If you feel a sense of hopelessness, trust is often absent.

It seems like a big step to choose to trust Me at times.

But as you do, your heart is filled with My hope, which by the power of My Spirit overflows in you.

You will find that I am trustworthy, My child.

Remember the times I have shown this to you, and your trust in Me will return to you more quickly.

You are so used to doing things all alone, and your journey has been heavy and painful at times.

You have been weary and lacking the energy you once had.

I am the answer to all of that.

When you trust Me, you recognize the truth: I am all-knowing, all-powerful, and all-loving.

Recognizing My truth is a first step to seeing and experiencing My hope right here in this hard place.

When you accept My truth, the result is always good for you and your future as you move forward with Me.

I don't wish for you to walk alone anymore.

Walk with Me, tell me of your hopes and dreams, your hurts and disappointments.

No area is too big or difficult for Me. I am not intimidated or worried about your current circumstance.

I see the end of your story. I see the next chapter. Knowing this, I have much encouragement for you if you'll choose to come to Me, listen, and share all that is in your heart.

I am your great counselor, better than the best life coach, your creator, and your friend. I am worthy of your trust today, My child.

Talk to Me about your day. Ask Me questions.

As you do this, you get to know more of Me and what I am like.

This will only increase your ability to truly trust Me with anything that comes your way.

There are good times ahead as we walk together in vulnerability and trust."

TRUST

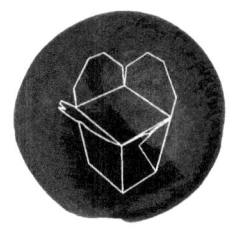

— Take Aways —

The greater my intimacy with God, the greater the confidence and trust I know I can have in Him.

Trust is about saying, "I am letting go of my 'right' to control, my ability to be independent of You, and choosing to put my hand in Yours with this area of my life."

IF I CAN TRUST, HOPE IS PRESENT.

God is willing to allow me to discover His trustworthiness—bit by bit or chunks at a time.

Trust, when given freely, brings freedom with it.

My trust levels have a direct correlation to my knowing the Father.

GOD IS TRUSTWORTHY EVERY TIME!

God's voice always reflects His nature. (Look at Jesus' example if you're unsure; the Son always reveals the Father.)

God loves the process as much as the result. The practice of trusting Him is a lifelong endeavour. Every time I choose to trust delights His heart.

TRUST

What if trust was a golden currency for God? What if my trust gave God permission to do immeasurably more than I could think of, ask for, or imagine? What would this look like in my situation?

GOD'S NATURE IS TRUSTWORTHY.

My natural state is limited, but when placed in His safe hands, I find that far more is possible.

God never rushes or demands me to trust Him. I can choose to believe in His ability or not.

I can choose to trust or to rule by myself; I cannot do both at the same time.

Hard seasons challenge my ability to trust…but what if I view this difficult space as an opportunity to trust, instead of a "should" trust situation, a "get-to" situation. One has a thread of hope. Which will I align myself with today?

— *Questions to Ponder* —

1. Was anything highlighted to me as I read through this chapter?

2. What helps me to trust someone? What characteristics do they need to possess?

3. Is there anything that makes trusting difficult for me? Why or why not?

> Whoever dwells in the shelter of the Most High will rest in the shadow of the Almighty. I will say of the LORD, "He is my refuge and my fortress, my God in whom I trust."
>
> **PSALM 91:1-2 NIV**

154 CHAPTER SEVEN

4. What part of how I view or experience this season needs some hope, uplifting, or tweaking? Am I willing to release my experiences—my past and any broken beliefs to Him?

5. What do I believe about trust? Do I believe any lies about this?

> I will save you; you will not fall by the sword, but will escape with your life, because you trust in me, declares the Lord.
>
> **JEREMIAH 39:18 NIV**

TRUST

6. Am I willing to open myself up for something fresh from Him as I choose to trust Him today? What advantages could this bring to my circumstance?

7. If trusting God is about submitting my right and ownership of something to Him, what areas might this impact? How much does my life reflect this now? Do I see anything that needs to change?

> Trust in the LORD with all your heart, and do not lean on your own understanding, in all your ways, acknowledge Him, and He will make your paths straight.
>
> **PROVERBS 3:5 - 6 NASB**

8. How was Jesus' trust in Father God evident in the Word? What were the benefits of Jesus' choosing to trust? Were there any disadvantages?

9. What would the implications of trusting possibly do for my circumstances and mindset?

> The king was overjoyed and gave orders to lift Daniel out of the den. And when Daniel was lifted from the den, no wound was found on him, because he had trusted in his God.
>
> **DANIEL 6:23 NIV**

TRUST

— *Trust Playlist* —

Trust in You – Lauren Daigle

I Will Trust – Elevation Worship

Cornerstone – Hillsong

Oceans – Hillsong

Turn Your Eyes upon Jesus - Helen Howarth Lemmel 1922

Do It Again – Mack Brock, Travis Cottrell

It Is Well – Horatio Spafford
(The Audrey Assad version is beautiful.)

Sovereign – Chris Tomlin

By the Grace of God – Bethel Music & Brian Johnson

— *Activations* —

MUSICAL

Soak in some trust declarational worship. Let the lyrics pierce your heart. Find one of your favourites or use one from the playlist on the previous page.

VISUAL

Read Scriptures which talk about the benefits of trusting God. Visually express one of these verses artistically. Let the colors used reflect the heart sense of these truths coming to fruition in your life.

LOGICAL

Ponder the two truths. Your physical reality vs. God's viewpoint of your current season.

Assuming God's truth trumps the natural world, what happens if you walk in one and not the other? Is it possible to walk in both? What is the outcome of walking each way? How would walking in God's truth impact your tough season?

KINESTHETIC/BODILY

Move your body along a narrow edge. Examples might be, the roadside edge, garden sleeper.

As you take one step at a time, declare your trust in God about an element of your current circumstance. E.g., "I trust You, God, with____." When you sense the peace of God within your body, take a look back at how far each step of trust has brought you.

INTRAPERSONAL

Is it possible to choose a higher realm by trusting? Saying no to what you feel, see, or experience in your own humanity? How open are you to the mystery of walking with Holy Spirit through tough? What could this look and feel like? Consider trust. How is trust evidenced in your life? In what/who do you place trust?

VERBAL

Ponder the situations where God has shown Himself trustworthy in your life. Journal with God, sharing any disappointments and hurts you've experienced. God is not frightened by your questioning and processing. He longs to restore relationships and build trust. Take some time to lament any unresolved tough seasons or circumstances. God loves your authenticity and vulnerability. No need for pretending everything is okay when its not. He longs to walk with you through this time.

INTERPERSONAL

Ask God to highlight areas He wants you to choose to trust afresh to Him. Talk with a safe friend or a mentor about the implications of choosing to trust. How does this choice impact hopes and dreams? Pray about these with your friend or with God Himself.

NATURALISTIC

Find a mature tree in your neighbourhood. Explore the roots systems and how broad their reach.

Consider the symbolism of trust between trunk, roots, and branches. Ask God to reveal a truth about trust through this experience.

Bless You

Be blessed, one who readily places his or her trust in the trustworthy One.

I bless you with the security of knowing how much you are loved by Him.

Bless you…with the assurance of knowing He is worthy of your trust.

Bless your heart with healing from those times your trust has been broken, abused, or misused.

Be blessed as you process past hurts, as you are heard, validated, and held by Him as you share with Him.

I bless your mind with ideas and inspiration about what you can trust God with today.

Be blessed as you dwell in the safety of the Lord Most High, resting in the shadow of His wings.

Bless you…with the experience of having God as your refuge and fortress.

Bless your body with the surety that comes from experiencing God's trustworthiness.

Be blessed as you trust in Him and your paths are made straight.

I bless your hardship journey with the ability to place your trust in healthy, honouring safe hands.

I bless your life with the freedom to trust.

Be blessed with all the benefits which come from placing your hand in His and learning to trust Him at every turn.

In Jesus' trustworthy and honourable name,

Amen.

xxxxx

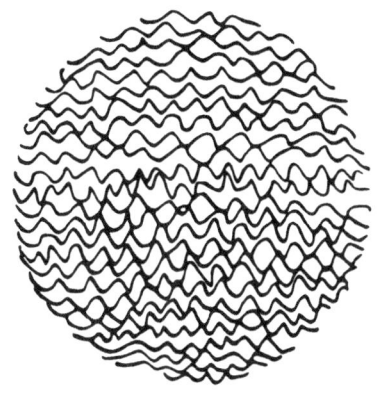

Chapter Eight

KINDNESS

— Father's Heart —

"You expect so much more of yourself than I do, My child.

You run here and there, pushing yourself to the limits of your human capacity.

You think little of Me or My strength that is fully available to you in it all.

You do this because your culture says being independent is a strength that brings you success.

I tell you now that your culture's message is a lie.

Being independent is a sign of weakness.

It takes a strong person to share his or her life with another and, more than that, to be honest in love and vulnerability.

The greatest type of love is to love others as yourself.

I long for My children to stop and take time to soak in Me and then go out into the world with My resources flowing with My Spirit.

Traveling in partnership with Me is the most incredible way to live.

You choose to run yourself to the point of exhaustion. Having nothing in reserve makes it hard to help those I put along your path—let alone yourself.

So be kind to yourself.

Take care of My temple: rest and eat well.

Actively ask Me how your life can be transformed from old to new.

The new life I provide is one of freedom.

If you are not looking after yourself and are too busy to listen, how will you have anything in reserve to invest in others?

Model this self-care to your family.

Let your children experience a healthy model—a healthy present Mum. You represent Me well when you love these little ones in this way. What will they learn from you? What legacy do you wish to leave them with?

Nurture yourself by coming to Me. Allow Me to reveal the good physical, mental and spiritual health available to you at this time.

You do this always by coming to Me and allowing Me to guide you in these healthy ways. You are not to make self-care an idol, instead a healthy life practice. It honors Me as you flow with My plans for your health.

My Son modeled this to you. He went up the mountain to pray and rest.

He took time to sit and be still, rather than busying Himself with the never-ending needs of people and physical tasks around Him.

He did this with a kingdom outlook and therefore is a perfect model.

I care about you, and therefore you should care about yourself.

Ask Me how I see you, and I will reflect it to your heart.

You are worthy of love. You are worth My attention.

If you allow yourself a healthy amount of love and care, you will love others from a place of health. Love out of an abundance of My love, which you will know for yourself.

You can't give away what you have not experienced, My beloved one."

KINDNESS

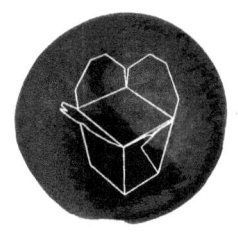

— Take Aways —

Ensuring my body is getting what it needs in life is like servicing a vehicle. I can continue to drive, but if I never put fuel in the tank or service the worn-out parts, the engine will seize up, proving a costly decision.

People will always have needs; I am not their answer—Jesus is!

I AM WORTHY OF LOVE. I AM WORTHY OF HIS ATTENTION.

When I choose to continually push through at the cost of my health, I am not honouring the body God gave me.

Looking after myself is non negotiable.

Boundaries are required if I hope to have capacity in my tank.

God values me and says I have great worth—not less or more than anybody else. My own unique value gifted from the Creator.

God wants me to tend to the place where Holy Spirit resides, including His temple within me.

It takes a strong person to share his or her life in vulnerability, honesty, and love.

GOD EXPECTS LESS OF ME THAN I DO OF MYSELF AT TIMES.

Sometimes I can place more value upon others than myself.

I sense that you and I need to read this: "It is okay to be kind to myself."

KINDNESS

JESUS MODELED HEALTHY SELF-CARE.

It honors God when I choose to flow with Holy Spirit and His promptings. He can show me the best balance of self and others.

By saying yes to every "good thing," I am possibly saying no to God's best.

If I choose to neglect myself, then I'll have nothing in reserve for others.

I am often "kinder to those around me than I am to myself."

God is so kind to me. Why do I struggle to be kind to myself at times?

If I want to flourish, I must be willing to let go of things I "should" be doing to make way for whatever God knows will fit me best.

— *Questions To Ponder* —

1. Am I kind to myself? What advantages has this consideration brought to my life? Have these also been advantageous to others? How?

   _____
   _____
   _____
   _____
   _____
   _____
   _____
   _____

2. What would life be like if I lived according to my God design, rather than what the world commands? Is there a difference? What brings me greater peace? Is there a way to flourish in both?

   _____
   _____
   _____

KINDNESS

3. Is there a correlation between my identity and being able to care for others? Do I have a healthy balance in these areas?

> Jesus said to him, "Love the Lord your God with all your heart, with all your soul, and with all your mind." This is the first and greatest commandment. The second is like it, "love your neighbor as yourself."
>
> **MATTHEW 22:38-39 NET**

4. What beliefs do I have about looking after or prioritizing self? Is this easy or difficult to do? Why or why not?

5. Do I place value upon my life? Do I value others better than myself? Ponder these questions with God. Ask Him about my worth and value.

> In everything, therefore, treat people the same way you want them to treat you, for this is the Law and the Prophets.
>
> **MATTHEW 7:12 NASB**

6. Are there any lies that I believe about being kind to myself? If so, what is God's truth?

7. How do I interpret these words of Jesus in Mark 12:30-31? How do I come to peace between the tension of being servant-hearted and also loving myself?

> Indeed, no one ever hated his own body, but he nourishes and cherishes it, just as Christ does the church.
>
> **EPHESIANS 5:29 BSB**

8. What emotions do I feel when I take the time to be kind to myself? Share both positive and negative.

9. Do I find it difficult to say no? Why or why not? Ask some questions of God and self about any beliefs I have about saying no.

> I will give thanks to you because I have been so amazingly and miraculously made. Your works are miraculous, and my soul is fully aware of this.
>
> **PSALM 139:14 GWT**

KINDNESS

10. Is there anything holding me back from being kind to myself? What is God saying? (The answers might reveal much about how I perceive and encounter the nature of God in my current space.)

11. What are the consequences of failing to be kind to myself? What are the advantages of addressing this necessity in my life? Are there others who would benefit from my choice of being kind to myself?

For everything created by God is good, and nothing is to be rejected if it is received with gratitude.

1 TIMOTHY 4:4 NAS 1977

12. Understanding that there are seasons of giving and receiving, what would life look and feel like if I chose to do whatever is necessary to bless my body, mind, heart? What does my body, heart and mind need most at this time? (Refer to appendix 4, page 349 for more insight)

KINDNESS

— Be Kind to Yourself Playlist —

Lost in Your Love – Brandon Lake ft. Sarah Reeves House of Miracles

Shepherd Boy – Chris Tomlin

I Can See Clearly Now – Jimmy Cliff

Be Kind to Yourself – Andrew Peterson

Burn Bright – Natalie Grant

Lord, I Need You – Matt Maher

Flawless – Mercy Me

Dear Younger Me – Mercy Me

— Activations —

MUSICAL

Write a verse or a song which reflects God's kindness toward you in this season.

VISUAL

Create a "Be Kind to Myself" chart. Visually represent all the things that invest in your love tank and build capacity in your energy stores. Ask God to reveal times where you can prioritise these in your calendar. The next time you get a prompt, you have a visual reminder of what fills your tank.

LOGICAL

What does God say about being kind to yourself? How does He encourage us to take care of ourselves? Did Jesus have boundaries? Explore any Bible passages that reveal His heart about this.

Ask God for any revelations of truth which are applicable for your own circumstance.

KINDNESS

KINESTHETIC/BODILY

Kick off your shoes and go for a walk in the grass. Enjoy the peace. Let go of all the thoughts which distract you from being present with God. Enjoy the springy feel of the grass beneath your feet. Consider the softness of God's arms as He tends to you in this time.

INTRAPERSONAL

Start a conversation with God about what life could look and feel like, with choosing only those things that He ordains. Ask Him to encounter what it brings to your life if you lived with this in mind. Enjoy some time together.

VERBAL

Write your own list of life-givers and life takers. Assume that your calendar is cleared. If you could build a dream calendar where everything scheduled is what you love, what would it look like? How would it be different? Ponder how more of these can be applied to your life today.

INTERPERSONAL

Are the people in your life making it easier or more difficult to say yes or no to things? Are there some boundaries that need to be established or altered? Talk to God or a trusted counsellor or friend. Create some action plan steps to better manage this season, making it healthier for your life.

NATURALISTIC

Find a comfortable place to lie down and watch the clouds pass by. Rest. Be open to what God wants to say during this time. Consider the areas in Appendix 4 on page 349.

Bless You

Precious and greatly loved by Him one,

I bless you with freedom and permission to let go of old commitments that aren't designed for now.

Bless you... with insight and kingdom inspiration when it comes to knowing what kindness to yourself is like.

I bless you with the community you need at this time and ones who are for you—not against you.

Be blessed as you cherish and nourish your own body just as Christ does the church.

I bless you with a hunger to want what God wants more than what others or society desire.

I bless you with fresh eyes to see this as a new season with new strategies; the old doesn't necessarily fit here.

Bless your body and its systems with refreshing sleep.

I bless you with the revelation that you are worthy of love. You are worthy of His attention. You are worthy of kindness.

Be blessed with revelations of truth and that whatever you do, its purpose is to glorify God.

I bless you with the knowledge and experience that being kind to yourself today helps to equip and strengthen you for the tomorrows.

I bless you with the ability to see yourself as God sees you.

KINDNESS

Bless you with a contented heart because God created you, and you are created magnificently.

In the precious and beautiful name of Jesus.

Amen.

xxxxx

Chapter Nine

GOD'S CHARACTER

— Father's Heart —

"Oh, child, you see the Son, you see Me.

You hear the Son, you hear Me.

You love the Son, you love Me.

Whatever is true, whatever is honorable, lovely, admirable, loving, kind, good, or uplifting, think upon these things; I long to reveal Myself in greater measure to you.

Whatever reflects the Son and His heart reflects Me. (See Philippians 4:8.)

To know Me is to love Me. To love Me is to trust Me more deeply.

Just as I know you intimately, I long for you to know Me deeply.

There is much to uncover. You could spend a thousand lifetimes and still not come close to discovering all that I am.

This is the most excellent adventure you can go on in life is to get to know Me and My heart for the world.

Experiencing My nature's various aspects is not a dull task, but a fruitful and fun adventure.

These things change your daily life in impacting and wonderful ways.

Spend some time reading My Word and asking Me to reveal my heart within it, and you will encounter Me.

When you know Me, you know the truth, and the truth will set you free (John 8:32).

Getting to know Me will be the richest decision you'll ever make.

As you know Me, you will begin to see the world as I do. You'll see people as I do. Everything looks different through My sight.

Where before there seemed no way forward or out…with Me, I shower My hope upon you.

I am worthy of the time, worthy of the investment, and worthy of your heart. This is no small thing to choose to discover more of Me because there is always more.

Some journeys start and stop with you. This journey is a living, breathing thing that teaches and inspires, changes, shifts, and uplifts.

By learning about and encountering My heart, your inner world aligns with My heavenly heartbeat.

The world never looked so good when seen through the eyes of My heart."

GOD'S CHARACTER

— Take Aways —

Investing time, asking questions of God about Himself is one of the richest ways to spend time. It is a heavenly investment for today and eternity.

The greater I encounter God's heart, the increased faith I have in Him.

AS I SEE JESUS AND HIS HEART, I SEE AND EXPERIENCE WHO GOD IS.

He doesn't force me, but I "get to" know and love Him. It is my privilege to go on a journey of His heart and nature.

As I discover more about His personality and nature, intimacy grows between us.

Life is better for knowing that God is so much more than what I understand or experience of Him today.

The more I know and love God, the less the external circumstances shake and impact me.

The best of others' personalities reflects God's nature to me.

God loved me first. Nothing can be added to His love or taken away from it; He is fully whole and complete—not lacking anything.

THE FRUIT OF THE SPIRIT REFLECT HIS NATURE.

There is always more with God—depths I can leap into and swim about for millenniums to come.

GOD'S CHARACTER

I can sometimes look at God through my circumstances filter, which is tuned to pain, distress or memories of trauma. Yet His heart is to bring a balm and remedy. As I attune to Him, this happens naturally.

EVERY VERSE, EVERY PASSAGE, AND EVERY BOOK CAN REVEAL MORE OF GOD'S HEART.

Through this journey of discovery, truth is revealed. I "get to" walk with God and seek to abide in His truth—instead of the lies of the enemy.

Whatever is good, altogether lovely, powerful and true is His heart for me.

God wants to be discovered, known, and loved for who He is.

As I become confident in one aspect of God's nature, He can introduce another for me to encounter, ensuring I never become "familiar" with my great and Holy Father. Ensuring I will never tire of getting to know or experience Him.

— Questions To Ponder —

1. What leapt out to me as I was reading through this chapter?

2. What aspects of God's nature are most prevalent to me? How have I encountered God in my life story so far?

GOD'S CHARACTER

3. What has most influenced how I view God's nature and heart?

> He is the radiance of the glory of God and the exact imprint of his nature, and he upholds the universe by the word of his power. After making purification for sins, he sat down at the right hand of the Majesty on high.
>
> **HEBREWS 1:3 ESV**

4. How do I view God? As a harsh judge, lightning-bolt thrower, or as a loving, protective Father? Maybe both? Why or why not? What have I experienced which supports this viewpoint?

5. As I read the Bible, what stands out to me about God's nature?

> This is the message we have heard from Him and announce to you that God is Light, and in Him, there is no darkness at all.
>
> **1 JOHN 1:5 WEB**

GOD'S CHARACTER

6. Do I look at the natures of Father, Jesus, and Holy Spirit the same or differently? Do I connect more readily with one member more than another? Why? Ask Him for clarification if unsure.

7. As I look at my friends and family, what are their best characteristics?

> When I look at your heavens, the work of your fingers, the moon and the stars, which you have set in place, what is man that you are mindful of him, and the son of man that you care for him?
>
> **PSALM 8:3-4 ESV**

8. Is it possible that the good things that impact my heart is God revealing a snippet of something of Himself? How have I experienced this in my life?

9. Do I *want* to know more about God? Why or why not? How can I foster a growing experience of God's heart in my life?

> I knew that you are a gracious and compassionate God, slow to anger and abounding in love, a God who relents from sending calamity.
>
> **JONAH 4:2B NIV**

10. How can knowing more of God's heart and nature benefit me? What advantages can this bring to this hardship season?

Opposition to truth cannot be excused on the basis of ignorance, because from the creation of the world, the invisible qualities of God's nature have been made visible, such as his eternal power and transcendence. He has made his wonderful attributes easily perceived, for seeing the visible makes us understand the invisible. So then, this leaves everyone without excuse.

ROMANS 1:20 TPT

GOD'S CHARACTER

— *God's Character Playlist* —

You Are Worthy of It All – David Brymer and Onething

Revelation Song – Jesus Culture

You Are for Me – Kari Jobe

10,000 Reasons – Matt Redman

You Are So Good – Stairway Music

Above All – Lenny LeBlanc

All Hail King Jesus – Jeremy Riddle

Multiplied - NeedToBreathe

Where the light is - Dan Bremnes

CHAPTER NINE

— Activations —

MUSICAL

Spend some time in the psalms. What do they tell you about God's nature and heart?

VISUAL

Gather some paints/watercolors, art supplies. With Holy Spirit, create something which reflects part of His heart towards you. A couple of prompter questions might be: "God, who do You want to be for me today?" "What do You desire to bring me?"

LOGICAL

Many books and websites outline the various names of God. Select one. Now invest some time exploring the various names of God and their meanings. Reflect upon them, keeping note of aspects which are evident in your current situation. Thank God for those good gifts.

KINESTHETIC/BODILY

As you go to bed at night, be still before Him. When peace is evident, ask Holy Spirit to reveal something about Himself that you don't yet know. Wait in that restful place, attentive to whatever you sense, feel, hear, see, taste or think.

GOD'S CHARACTER

INTRAPERSONAL

Consider this truth: "He sees me. He knows me. He was there when I lost my first tooth, kissed my first love, and shed my first tear." What implications does seeing God like this have for your current situation? How does this make you feel? How can you engage with God in this way?

VERBAL

Before reading the Bible, ask God to show you something about Himself through whatever you are reading. As you read, watch or listen, and look out for aspects of God's nature that are being highlighted. (Remember I see the Son; I see the Father.) Write your own psalm of hardship and then listen for and write down God's response.

INTERPERSONAL

In conversation with safe people, ask them what they believe to be God's most precious trait.

Be inquisitive. Ask how they know this about Him? Are there any stories which display these? Thank these people for their willingness to share. Testimonies build faith in one another that help us to see aspects of God which might be needed. It also invests hope and faith in both, the sharer and the listener.

NATURALISTIC

Go for a gentle stroll, asking God to reveal aspects of His heart through His creation. What does nature sing about God's personality?

— Bless You —

I bless you with fresh insight into God's nature.

I bless you as you have new encounters with God's heart.

Be blessed with dreams filled with revelations of His heart for you.

*I bless you with the words of the Bible coming
alive with His personality and depths.*

*Bless you…with eyes to see Jesus' being a whole and complete representative
of God here on earth, encompassing all aspects of His beautiful nature.*

Be blessed with a desire to draw nearer to Him because of who He is.

I bless you with eyes to see His heart in everyday circumstances and situations.

Bless you…with the ability to see God's heart in the actions of others.

I bless your heart with an attunement to His.

*I bless you with the ability to see the loving, gentle, and
kind elements of God's heart for you at this time.*

*Be blessed with an expansion of the current tent pegs of
your understanding and experience of God's heart.*

*Be blessed with an increase in vision, heart, and hope
as your hardship meets God's redemptive heart.*

In Jesus' wholly perfect personality, nature and name,

Amen.

xxxxx

Chapter Ten

LISTENING

— Father's Heart —

"My child, scurrying, hurrying, busy, busy, busy. All this activity sometimes fills your ears so that you don't notice My voice.

I long to live in effortless communication with you.

Speaking and listening to one another in pure intimacy. My heart is for you to hear My voice and know Me fully.

I have much to say to you. I have many mysterious and wonderful truths to share with you. I have all this and more for you.

I desire to commune with you because I love you.

You can walk through life without Me, but I desire something greater for you.

I won't ever force you to hear Me.

I wait, ready for the moment when you turn to Me and talk to Me about the things of your depths.

Even when you don't turn to Me, I have gentle words of life ready for you if you'd choose to listen.

My words are not ever burdensome or heavy. My words are comforting, secure, and sure.

I am your safe place, and My words are for you because I love you.

*I have words of life to share with you. Words
that are for yours and others' good.*

My voice sounds like the fruit of the Spirit.

*Are the words you hear loving, joyful, peaceful, patient,
kind, good, gentle, faithful, or full of self-control?*

*These are the things you have to look forward
to, as you choose to meet with Me.*

Tuning your ears to My heartbeat for you and the world.

I know that you have many voices of experts and those who wish to help.

*Listen to Me first and foremost. I will show you the way
through the minefield of advice. I will not lead you astray.*

My words are trustworthy and insightful because truth always is.

*I am Truth. I am also Love. So you have no need to fear what I
have to say to you. You are My precious child, whom I love. My
words will be like honey to your soul and light to your spirit.*

Come, rest in Me.

*Ask Me to show you what is going on. Ask Me questions about all that
concerns you. Then wait and watch for My peace to invade. Infiltrating
any heaviness and bringing you something fresh and life-giving.*

Are you tired? Are you weary? Do you long to let everything go and just be?

Let Me be your compass. Your North Star—your guide.

There is none like Me.

I desire for you to have life and life to the full.

*Come, let's walk awhile, and I will tell you about hidden
things yet unknown to you. Prepare to be amazed!"*

LISTENING

— Take Aways —

As I let go of my agendas and lists and simply be with Him, the more I hear His voice of truth. His truth often speaks to the heart of the very things that concerned me.

He has celebrated with me, delighted in me, and enjoyed the moments where a single word of His opens a world of hope.

Practicing the art of listening enables me to capture God's vision and then love myself and others with what He has given.

LEARNING TO LISTEN TO GOD FOSTERS A NATURAL PEACE AND REST STATE.

God has something to say to me right now. I need only to stop long enough to become aware of Him and ask what He wants to say or do.

Through listening, He has comforted me, tended to me, and blessed my heart, especially during difficult times.

God is my safe place, my comforter, my friend in troubled times.

Listening says, "I want to know Your heart, Lord. Attune my ears to Your voice."

LEARNING TO LISTEN PLACES GOD ABOVE ALL ELSE.

God's words are ALWAYS life-giving, truthful, kind, gentle, encouraging, and for my good. I have no need to fear when I take the time to listen to God.

LISTENING

God's voice can sound like my own. He speaks in ways that I can understand. For me, His voice is often like a calming inner voice—not a loud, booming voice from the skies. His is a voice that carries His presence with it.

LISTENING SETS THE TONE FOR ABIDING IN HIS PRESENCE.

Listening leads me into a space of rest and posture of "Be still."

He is my compass for knowing the next step in this journey.

Listening to God is a revelatory space where things unknown or unseen are revealed, lifting me to higher, better places.

Experiencing God's nature and His heart can be through Him personally speaking to me. Whenever I experience the fruit of His Spirit, this too, might be Him speaking. Whatever reflects Him is His voice.

— *Questions to Ponder* —

1. Did any specific words/phrases leap out for me in today's reading?

2. How do I hear God? How does He speak to me? What does God's voice sound like to me?

LISTENING

3. How do I recognize that God is speaking and not me or the enemy? In my experience, what are the differences?

> But he who enters by the door is the shepherd of the sheep. To him, the gatekeeper opens. The sheep hear his voice, and he calls his own sheep by name and leads them out. When he has brought out all his own, he goes before them, and the sheep follow him, for they know his voice.
>
> JOHN 10:24 ESV

4. Are there any stumbling blocks to my hearing Him?

5. How easy or difficult do I find it to listen? What helps me to listen better? (refer to Appendix 5, page 351 for further inspiration.)

> Call to me, and I will answer you and tell you great and unsearchable things you do not know.
>
> **JEREMIAH 33:3 NIV**

LISTENING

6. What do I believe about hearing God's voice?

7. Is any part of me overwhelmed, nervous or fearful of hearing God's voice?

> And the Lord came and stood, calling as at other times, "Samuel! Samuel!" And Samuel said, "Speak, for your servant hears.
>
> **1 SAMUEL 3:10 ESV**

CHAPTER TEN

8. What advantages are there in learning how to hear God's voice for myself?

9. When have I previously encountered God? How have I heard Him communicate already?

> My sheep listen to my voice; I know them, and they follow me. I give them eternal life, and they will never perish. No one can snatch them away from me.
>
> **JOHN 10:27-28 NLT**

LISTENING

10. Have I been warned about something and failed to listen? How do I see this experience looking back? What could I learn from it?

11. What benefits would hearing God's voice bring to my current circumstance?

> Make me to know your ways,
> O LORD; teach me your paths.
> Lead me in your truth and
> teach me, for you are the
> God of my salvation; for you,
> I wait all the day long.
>
> **PSALM 25:4-5 ESV**

My child, listen to what I say,
and treasure my commands.
Tune your ears to wisdom,
and concentrate on understanding.
Cry out for insight,
and ask for understanding.
Search for them as you would for silver;
seek them like hidden treasures.
Then you will understand what it means to fear the Lord,
and you will gain knowledge of God.

PROVERBS 2:1-5 NLT

LISTENING

— Listening Playlist —

Way Maker – Sinach

Dear God – Cory Asbury

I Want to Know You – Paul McClure

Here's My Heart – Lauren Daigle

Rescue – Lauren Daigle

I Choose to Worship – Rend Collective

Listening to You – Morgan Elissa Grace

Have My Heart – Maverick City ft. Chandler Moore & Chris Brown

— Activations —

MUSICAL

Select a piece of instrumental music. Ask God to show you more of Himself while it is playing.

Try being present in the moment. Take note of any ideas, feelings, pictures which might "randomly" come to mind.

VISUAL

Consider how God spoke to people in the Bible. Think upon God's heart and how He desires to be heard by you. Create some images which reflect the ways God can speak. Ask Him to reveal how He wants to speak to you today.

LOGICAL

Note down the various ways that God has spoken to you, understanding that whenever we experience God's nature and His heart, He can be His speaking to us. What do you notice about these expressions of Him? Are there more available for you to encounter?

KINESTHETIC/BODILY

Go to a place with sand or another impressionable material. Listen for what God is revealing to you through the sand. Become aware of your senses and the thoughts which zip in.

INTRAPERSONAL

Spend some time listening. Initially, this exercise might be challenging. Journal any thoughts. As ideas come in, jot them down—God ideas and even distractions. Record all thoughts. When a particularly interesting idea comes in, ask a question. Then listen for the answer/response that comes.

VERBAL

Ask God, "What do You want to say to me, Lord?" Take note of the very first thing that you hear, sense, feel, observe. Try not to second-guess yourself; just write down what comes. Ask follow-up questions based on the first thought.

INTERPERSONAL

Spend some time with a good friend or a family member in prayer. Have them ask questions of God as you simply listen for His responses. You might collate a few questions together beforehand that relate to your current circumstance. It's always good to start with yes/no questions or asking for pictures.

NATURALISTIC

Go to a favourite place in nature. Close your eyes and simply listen. Distinguish the different sounds and their sources. Now try a deeper level of listening beyond what the human ear can hear. Using the hearing of your heart, ask God what He wants to share in this time together.

— Bless You —

I bless you, one who has ears to hear and a heart that connects with the One who knows and loves you best.

I bless you with a desire to hear God clearly for yourself.

I bless you with a greater sensitivity to God's voice and heart.

I bless you with a greater peace about whether you hear God.

I bless you with the ability to step into rest, over striving.

Bless you…with an attunement to God's discernment and wisdom.

Be blessed with being able to call out to God, so that He can show you great and unsearchable things not yet known.

I bless you with the ability to read and interpret all that God is showing you.

Bless you…with the ability to take note of those gentle promptings and to follow them.

I bless you with the ability to understand your body's messages but be governed by God's promptings.

Be blessed by Him as you hear His heart and desire for you today.

In Jesus' ever-attentive name,

Amen.

XXXXX

Chapter Eleven

GOD'S PRESENCE

— Father's Heart —

"My presence is My gift to you, child.

It is a heavenly gift that not only speaks, encourages, and lifts you but is a powerful tool for changing what is seen. Align it to My way of seeing things: the truth.

As you choose to travel with Me throughout your day, My presence goes with you—the greater your awareness of Me, the more you see My hand of influence in your day.

Be still before Me, asking Me to awaken and expand the awareness you have of Me.

I will not disappoint you, precious child of Mine. Being in My presence requires your trust, but it will be well worth it.

I long to reveal more of Myself to you.

My presence is the essence of My nature in a tangible form. It's just one way that you can feel Me and know I am real.

I can be felt, sensed, and depended upon. I am greater than any double-edged sword for bringing down anything that doesn't align with Me and My ways.

My presence can do all this and so much more. I am limitless as to what I can do.

My ways are always for your good.

*Do not be afraid of My presence. I will only
give you as much as you can take in.*

*I know and love you so well. I won't ever put you in a
place that I have not also resourced you for.*

*As you walk with Me and become more aware of Me in your day, you
will find that My very nature invades all you are involved with.*

Things that used to burden you are no longer heavy.

*You once had no patience for people; you now
find the gold in them—because of Me.*

Acknowledge My presence in difficult places.

*Choose to believe in Me and My capacity, rather than only what is
seen. And I will shift all that looks to oppose My plans in and for you.*

My presence is an invitation for intimacy with Me.

*It is My way of sharing who I am with you, from a place of strength and
vulnerability. I will teach you My ways through your awareness of Me.*

I love it when we spend time together and enjoy being with one another.

I enjoy you, My beloved.

Life can sometimes burden you beyond what I desire for you.

*When you walk in the awareness of My presence,
you live lightly, freely, and in joy.*

*Walking with Me is never dull; it is always a
purposeful and fully satisfying adventure.*

Let's have some fun together today."

GOD'S PRESENCE

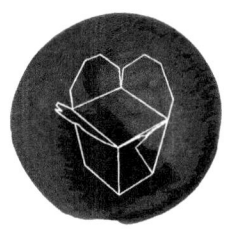

— *Take Aways* —

God's presence is a gift to me.

He is high above all that looks to crush me. God's presence lifts my eyes to His truth.

HIS PRESENCE IS A GAME CHANGER FOR LIFE.

It's the place where all human limitations are left behind, and heavenly vision is adopted.

God's presence is the place where heaven and earth touch, then embrace.

Fostering an awareness of God's presence increases my experience of His nature.

God's presence is an opportunity for intimacy with Him.

God's presence allows me to walk lightly even when things look bleak.

I CAN CHOOSE TO PARTNER WITH HIS PRESENCE AT ANY MOMENT.

As I invite God in, each situation, mindset, or belief I have can be turned on its head in a moment.

GOD'S PRESENCE

It's within His presence that I encounter and experience His pure heart of love for me.

IN HIS PRESENCE, I COME FACE TO FACE WITH MY FATHER.

His presence lights up the parts of Him in me. Nothing else can stand up in the light of His presence.

God can plant or plow seeds through His presence—no matter how fragile I might be.

When walking through hard places, His presence is the balm and the strength. Through His presence, whatever I need at any moment can be connected with.

— *Questions to Ponder* —

1. What aspects of today's chapter jumped out to me?

2. What is God's presence like? How do I know I am encountering God's presence?

GOD'S PRESENCE

3. What are my beliefs about God's presence? What has been my experience with His presence?

> Let us then with confidence draw near to the throne of grace, that we may receive mercy and find grace to help in time of need.
>
> **HEBREWS 4:16 ESV**

4. What does God's Word tell me about His presence?

5. It could be said that God's presence is encountering the very heart of Him. What impact might this perception have in all areas of my life?

> That times of refreshing may come from the presence of the Lord.
>
> **ACTS 3:20A ESV**

GOD'S PRESENCE

6. He is not limited by anything I am experiencing. What area of my life do I desire His presence to infiltrate today?

7. Where do I need a little more of Him and a little less of everything else?

> And he said, "My presence will go with you, and I will give you rest."
>
> **EXODUS 33:14 ESV**

8. Does anything hinder me from encountering more of God's presence?

9. Am I aware of any parts of me that are off limits to God? Why? What does God say about this?

> You make known to me the path of life; in your presence, there is fullness of joy; at your right hand are pleasures forevermore.
>
> **PSALM 16:11 BSB**

10. What benefits would there be in becoming more aware of inviting God's presence into my situations? For myself? For my health? For others?

Behold, I stand at the door and knock.
If anyone hears my voice and opens the door,
I will come in to him and eat with him,
and he with me.

REVELATION 3:20 ESV

GOD'S PRESENCE

— *God's Presence Playlist* —

Nothing Else – Cody Carnes

Spirit Move – Kalley Heiligenthal

Spirit of God – Phil Wikham

Here as in Heaven – Mack Brock/Steven Furtick/Elevation Worship

Holy Spirit – Jesus Culture (I love Francesca Battistelli version.)

Spirit Break Out – Kim Walker-Smith

In Your Presence – Jesus Culture

My Weapon – Natalie Grant

Rainbow – Kacey Musgraves

There are also some amazing instrumentals for helping us to connect with His presence.

CHAPTER ELEVEN

— Activations —

MUSICAL

Spend some time worshipping; welcome God's presence as you commune with Him.

Respond however you sense to. Check out the playlist or there are some amazing instrumentals for helping us to connect with His presence.

VISUAL

Work with your favourite art materials and create a visual representation of God's presence. Or how you feel when encountering God's presence.

LOGICAL

Spend some time reflecting upon Jesus' life. What biblical examples can you find of Jesus encountering God's presence? What evidence is there of this? Were there aspects of God's presence Jesus carried continuously? How would you explain the relationship between God's presence and Jesus?

KINESTHETIC/BODILY

How will you recognize His presence when it comes? Some experience Him through peace, through heat, tingling or increasing joy. Encountering God's presence is unique for each one. Ask God for an experience of His presence. Pay attention to what is happening in the parts of your body, mind, and the atmosphere around you.

INTRAPERSONAL

The next time you feel a weight that isn't yours to carry, ask God to show you what to do with it. Then ask Holy Spirit to fill that space with His presence. Take note of what happens internally and then externally.

VERBAL

Write a thank-you letter to God. Articulate all that God's presence has brought to your life.

Bless God in your own uniquely personal way. Not a time for requests, but a time of gratefulness for who God is.

INTERPERSONAL

Explore the connection between God's nature and God's presence. How are they different? How are they the same? How are they connected? Why is this important to know? Consider how what you've uncovered might impact your intimacy with God.

NATURALISTIC

Spend some time in a favourite place outside, thanking God. Ask Him for an encounter with His presence in this place.

— Bless You —

I bless you, precious one, whom God cherishes.

I bless you with a revelation of God's wholeness and greatness.

Be blessed as you draw near to Him, He draws near to you.

I bless you with a desire to fearlessly encounter God's presence for yourself.

*Bless you…with refreshing, rest, and fullness
of joy as you encounter His presence.*

*I bless you with experiencing God's presence even
when walking through the depths of life.*

Bless your heart with softness and the ability to be molded by Him.

Bless you…with a desire to abide in God's presence.

*I bless you with the revelation of how God's presence
improves whatever is happening around or within you.*

*I bless you with understanding a sliver of the resources
God has put at your disposal through His presence.*

*Bless you…with experiencing the beautiful
rhythm of life when traveled with Him.*

Be blessed as you welcome connection with God through His presence.

In Jesus' name,

Amen.

XXXXX

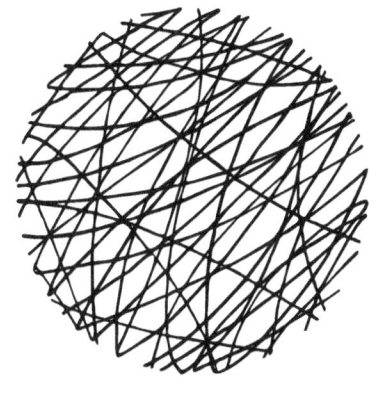

Chapter Twelve

PRAYER

— Father's Heart —

"Come to Me; talk to Me. This is prayer.

Don't be fooled into thinking of prayer as a ritual or just another item on your spiritual to-do list.

Prayer is simply time spent with Me:

Talking with Me,

Listening to Me,

Dreaming with Me,

Asking questions of Me,

Receiving from Me, and

Interceding on behalf of another.

It's where we meet in relationship. It's our time together to work things out and commune.

It's where you come in heavy laden, and you leave lighter and refreshed.

Prayer is the life source of relationship with Me.

Many have misrepresented prayer. The Enemy would have you believe it is tiring, boring, and a pointless ritual of religion.

I say prayer is the ultimate act of faith. Praying in faith is restorative, healing, comforting, and connecting. It's an opportunity to unite with Me in My heartbeat for you and the world around you.

My Word is powerful.

My Word is truth.

My Word is counter-cultural.

My Word is absolute.

My Word and story are an adventure—never boring or dull.

Prayer is your chance to discover who I am within the word and in the world.

It's the place where your heart and Mine entwine and unite.

Where you come to Me, and I reveal My heart to you—a space where you and others flourish because of having chosen to converse with Me.

At times we will talk about circumstances, problems, and people. I will bring My solutions to and through you, changing the world as a result.

I reveal Myself and My will to you through prayer.

Then you can declare and release My heart for that situation, having engaged with Me in relationship.

Through our times together, you will have the gift of being tended to by Me during difficult times.

You will discover the deep, abiding satisfaction that can only come through experiencing divine relationship as you grow in intimacy with Me.

You will encounter the delight of seeing things come to pass, just as I do.

PRAYER

You will know the power behind prayer and that I answer every single one through this time of abide.

Come to Me, child, put your heart before Me.

Now listen, as I reveal to you My heart for it all—for you.

Then you can pray with power and release, watching and experiencing all that I have to offer you.

You who choose to trust in Me to do immeasurably more than what you hear, feel, touch, taste, or see. Let me open up and unshackle the very things which have held you back from the power of connecting with Me through prayer.

I am broader, deeper, stronger, and higher than anything you might imagine.

Come, let's talk a while."

And pray in the Spirit on all occasions with all kinds of prayers and requests. With this in mind, be alert and always keep on praying for all the saints. Pray also for me, that whenever I open my mouth, words may be given me so that I will fearlessly make known the mystery of the gospel, for which I am an ambassador in chains. Pray that I may declare it as fearlessly as I should.

EPHESIANS 6:18-20 NIV

PRAYER

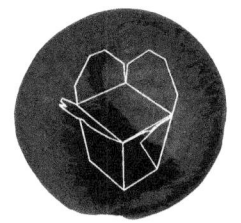

— Take Aways —

In prayer, God reveals Himself as loving, gracious, and kind. He is always life-giving, brings health, encouraging, uplifting, inspiring, healing, blessing, and responsive.

In prayer, I get to meet with my Creator, who knows and loves me intimately and wholeheartedly—without reservation.

Prayer is not dry and dull, but an honest, raw, and vulnerable space. In this place, my vulnerability is honored and increased.

Prayer is not complicated; it's simply an awareness and interaction with God.

PRAYER IS THE BEGINNING AND END OF ALL THINGS.

Prayer is intimate and personal, connecting Father and me.

Acknowledging Him in life fosters a growing awareness of my own thoughts, words and actions—and His interaction with these.

Prayer can bring a richness to life—much like a delicious meal with the variety of a full buffet spread.

Prayer is where the cries of my heart meet His ears, and He responds.

Prayer is the time when God speaks life into me.

PRAYER IS A GIFT— THE GIFT OF RELATIONSHIP.

Prayer doesn't stop and start; it can be an ongoing conversation with God.

As I bring my ideas, needs, questions, and cries to Him, He responds, proving Himself to be the final word for all my circumstances.

PRAYER

PRAYER HAS LIMITLESS POTENTIAL FOR CHANGING WHATEVER COMES.

Praying with others is POWERFUL, but nothing is better than praying with God for myself. There I have a voice and am empowered by Him in the process of meeting Him.

Prayer and life go together. With prayer, there is life.

As I step into conversation with Him, the greater my internal peace as any fear is minimised.

Prayer pours out, lifts up, shifts, moves, welcomes, invites, and so much more.

When I don't feel like praying, it's possibly the very thing that will help!

As I encounter who God is through prayer, I also get to adopt my God-given identity.

Asking Jesus what He is praying for on my behalf and being in agreement with Him is a great way to see my prayers answered with a resounding "Yes" every time.

— Questions to Ponder —

1. What elements of this chapter grabbed my attention?

2. Do I see prayer as an intimate conversation between the Creator and me? Or something else? How do I view prayer?

PRAYER

3. Is there any part of me that has mystified prayer, making it harder than it needs to be? If so, why?

> Therefore, I tell you, whatever you ask for in prayer, believe that you have received it, and it will be yours.
>
> **MARK 11:24 NIV**

4. How powerful is prayer to me? What do I believe about it?

5. How or when have I seen and experienced God answering prayer?

> Then Jesus told his disciples a parable to show them that they should always pray and not give up.
>
> **LUKE 18:1 NIV**

6. What connections are there between faith, belief, and prayer?

7. Is there a connection between how I view God and how I pray? If so, what is the connection and what impact does this have on the journey?

CHAPTER TWELVE

8. Do I desire to grow in how I communicate with God? Or am I comfortable in my current space? Do I believe there is more available to me through prayer? Why or why not?

9. What advantages would there be if I brought everything to God in prayer first? Would anything need to change for this to be a reality in my life?

> Do not be anxious about anything, but in everything by prayer and petition with thanksgiving, present your requests to God. And the peace of God, which transcends all understanding, will guard your hearts and minds in Christ Jesus.
>
> **PHILIPPIANS 4:6-7 NIV**

10. If there were no hindrances, what prayer would I love for God to answer in my life today? About what would I like to talk to God?

So I say to you, Ask, and it will be given to you; seek, and you will find; knock, and the door will be opened to you. For everyone who asks receives; he who seeks finds; and to him who knocks, the door will be opened. Which of you fathers, if your son asks for a fish, will give him a snake instead? Or if he asks for an egg, will give him a scorpion? If you then, though you are evil, know how to give good gifts to your children, how much more will your Father in heaven give the Holy Spirit to those who ask him!"

LUKE 11:9-13 NIV

PRAYER

— *Prayer Playlist* —

Awake My Soul – Hillsong worship

What a Friend We Have in Jesus – Joseph M. Scriven (words in 1855) and Charles Converse (music in 1868), Ireland

Loyal – Lauren Daigle

Soul's Anthem – Tori Kelly

The Prayer – Andrea Bocelli & Celine Dion

Every Victory – The Belonging Co. Danny Gokey

Open the Eyes of My Heart Lord – Paul Baloche

— Activations —

MUSICAL

Speak to and listen to God through instrumental, song, or freestyling creation. Let this time together be purely about connecting and being in awe of Him. Have no agenda but to be open to what He wants to do or bring. Enjoy!

VISUAL

Find a large jar. Each time something good happens, write it on a slip of paper and place it in your prayer container. At the end of the week, pour them out. Thank God for all of those good deposits. This can also be done with prayer requests. Taking note of your prayers can help you see the tangible answers God brings.

LOGICAL

Research and experiment with various methods of prayer. Take note of the connection with God during each time together. Observe which ways bring you a greater awareness of Him and His presence.

KINESTHETIC/BODILY

As you work with your hands, e.g., gardening, housework, building, etc., become aware of God in whatever you are doing. Try to be present and in the moment as you pull weeds or plant seeds. Endeavor to watch and listen for seemingly "random" ideas. Ask God a question, continue with your task, and wait for Him to reveal something.

INTRAPERSONAL

Consider your understanding and experience of how you communicate with God. What kind of relationship do you have with Him? How easy is it to share with Him all that is on your mind and heart? Spend some time now, journaling all that is on your mind to Him. Then be still, wait, listen, watch for His response.

VERBAL

Read through the psalms and take note of how David and God spoke to one another. Note whether David held back from God in His speech? How was he able to be honest and raw, but still honoring? How can David's style of communication help you in this current tough space? Consider how God and you communicate with one another.

INTERPERSONAL

Spend some time connecting with God. Pray for those people who don't yet know God personally for themselves. If you're unsure, ask God to bring people to mind. Even in hard places, you can bless the lives of others with your prayer.

NATURALISTIC

God is always saying something. As you go outside, stop and become aware of how He is speaking today. This can come in the form of words, gut feelings, "random events" or sensing. The list is endless in how He speaks. Keep watch for any themes or things which grab your attention. Then ask Him questions about them.

— Bless You —

Bless you…ones who can connect with God for themselves.

I bless you with clarity about what prayer is.

Bless you…with a heart for communicating with the Creator and Lover of your heart and design.

Be blessed with confidence in knowing that your prayers are heard and answered every time.

I bless you with a hunger for wanting a greater experience and revelation of God and His heart that hungers for time with Him.

Bless you…with knowing what to ask for, then seeking and finding what you are looking for. May the right doors open for you as you knock with the confidence the Lord gives you.

I bless you with the knowledge you are 100 percent safe when you are with God.

I bless you with encountering God's presence in your life, connecting and interacting with Him.

I bless you with a greater connection with God's heart, especially on tougher days.

I bless you that whatever comes your way, your first response will be to want to connect with God.

Bless you…with the experience of asking for things according to His will, knowing that you have what you ask for.

PRAYER

*Bless your mind with the ability to be settled
and able to step into God's peace.*

*I bless you with a natural conversation with the Lord, which
carries throughout the hours of your days and nights.*

In Jesus' ever-present, caring and attentive name,

Amen.

xxxxx

Chapter Thirteen

WEAKNESS

— Father's Heart —

*"My precious child, you were made to work
with Me in life and in relationship.*

If you are strong in all things, how would I show My power in your life?

If you have no need, how can I display My love for you through provision?

*If you are in control of all things, how can I interact with you
and create life-giving plans, bringing delight to us both?*

If you are good at all things, how will you experience My goodness?

*If I allowed you to walk through life without hardships,
how would your humility and awe of Me grow?*

Through these interactions, much happens.

Your faith grows from seed to tender root to large shady oak.

You grow in confidence in My ability to work in your life.

*You become accustomed to knowing when you need
to trust Me for the things you can't do alone.*

*I can show you the expanse of My love for you
when I make the impossible happen.*

Your weaknesses are the areas I choose to shine. My power manifests so you and others will see the supernatural nature of it and glorify Me.

All the while, your faith grows and is further cemented in Me.

You begin to learn the ebb and flow of My Spirit.

You experience more of My nature and the depth of My love for you. In your weaknesses I reveal the true nature of My heart for humankind: friendship with Me, weakness and strength, speaking and listening, hardship and breakthrough, hopelessness, and ultimate redemption.

I do not work as the world works. "What is sown in weakness is raised in power" (1 Corinthians 15:43).

Do not be surprised by circumstances that challenge, stretch, or confront you.

In these places, as you look to Me for answers and not at the circumstance, I reveal more of Myself and ways.

I will often use these situations to shape elements of your being that need honing to prepare you for what is to come. I don't necessarily send these difficulties, BUT I love to redeem the very thing sent to get you off track. I use it to help clear the path and open up the way forward.

I am always at work for, in, and through you.

I am patient with you, My precious child. If you do not get it the first time, I will encourage you to try again.

I do not see the failures and disappointments as you do; I only see fresh opportunities for growth and learning. The process is just as important as the end result to Me.

Nothing is wasted in Me.

WEAKNESS

This is the right way for you to look at things too.

Come to Me, child, when you are weak. Rest in Me, and I will give you what you need for that moment. Then you will turn to Me and give thanks.

You will become more aware of and turn to Me when challenges next arise.

You will depend on Me more freely and stand in awe of who I am and what I am able and willing to do for those who choose to love Me.

Nothing is impossible for Me and for those who are My children.

That includes you, My child, My beloved."

He gives strength to the weary, and to him who lacks might, He increases power. Though youths grow weary and tired, and vigorous young men stumble badly, yet those who wait for the Lord will gain new strength. They will mount up with wings like eagles; they will run and not get tired. They will walk and not become weary.

ISAIAH 40:29-31 NASB

WEAKNESS

— Take Aways —

When in strife, I can choose to run towards or away from God. Regardless of my choice, His arms are always open to me, ready to embrace me as I choose to turn towards Him.

My weakness can be the springboard for increased connection with God.

GOD DOES NOT BASE MY WORTH ON MY HUMAN ABILITY.

Vulnerability and openness can seem weak, and yet, in God's eyes, it is pure strength.

My weakness enables me to rely upon God and His capacity rather than my own.

Dependence upon myself can inadvertently cause me to live independently of Him.

I can claim nothing of what God does through me because it would all be impossible without Him.

God does not require my strength—only my heart.

If I have no lack, then how will I recognize my need for God?

NOTHING IS WASTED IN HIM.

God often provides for my weaknesses through my village—and I for them through Him.

God can fill the gap between what I am and what I need.

WEAKNESS

WHEN I PARTNER WITH HIS VISION RATHER THAN MY OWN, I AM FREE.

The greater my vulnerability with Him, the greater our intimacy. The more confident I become of His goodness and design for my life, the greater my hope.

As I embrace Him in my weakness over my troubles, intimacy grows.

God's desire is to meet my need as He already knows my need.

I am not limited by my weakness when I choose to walk with Him.

The greater my weakness, the greater my awareness of my need for Him.

God can resource me for whatever is needed in any given circumstance.

Weakness shared with safe people or as prompted by God gives others permission to share openly. The truth that we all have battles, strengths and weaknesses.

— *Questions to Ponder* —

1. Did anything specific jump out in this chapter?

2. What is it about weakness that I struggle with the most? Why?

WEAKNESS

3. Am I aware of my weaknesses? Those places where I need others? How do I respond to being in need? How easy is it for me to celebrate others' strengths when I am weak in those same areas?

> Therefore I am well content with weaknesses, with insults, with distresses, with persecutions, with difficulties, for Christ's sake, for when I am weak, then I am strong.
>
> **2 CORINTHIANS 12:10 NASB**

4. Have I considered the connection between intimacy with God and independence? How does this association apply to me today?

5. How would I feel if I knew that whatever I wasn't, God could be that for me? Does this make me feel better or worse about having need? Why do I think this is?

> To this end, I labor, struggling with all His energy, which so powerfully works in me.
>
> **COLOSSIANS 1:29 NIV**

6. Are there any stumbling blocks in front of my ability to let God or others into my vulnerable/weak spaces?

7. What do I need God to be for me today? How will I respond to God's provision?

8. What do I fear most about allowing my weakness to be seen?

9. Is there any way I can be more at ease with my own weakness?

10. "What do You wish to show me about this, Lord?"

11. What advantages would…

   a. Knowing my area of need bring?

   b. Sharing it with God bring?

c. Sharing it with others bring?

d. What would be the implications of letting go of the lie that we don't need others help? Or the lie that I can do it all on my own? Ask God about these questions one by one.

WEAKNESS

— Weakness Playlist —

It's Ok not to be Ok – Awaken Music

Graves into Gardens – Brandon Lake

You Are My Strength – Hillsong

Even When It Hurts – Hillsong United

His Strength Is Perfect – Stephen Curtis Chapman

Strength – Melissa Helser

O Lord – Lauren Daigle

I was carried – Roma Waterman

Sing it from the shackles – Rend Collective

— Activations —

MUSICAL

As you listen to "You Say" by Lauren Daigle, in worship, offer up your weaknesses symbolically to Him. Listen and wait for what He desires to impart.

VISUAL

Consider what God has been for you at this time. Create a memory stone or other physical symbol which marks God's provision for you in this season. Remembering His goodness to us on the hard days reminds us that He has done it before and can do it again.

LOGICAL

Research biblical characters who, in their weakness, received strength from the Lord. What was the problem? How did they respond to the problem? How was it resolved? What do these accounts reveal to you about yourself and God?

KINESTHETIC/BODILY

Endeavour to enter into vulnerability and take note of how He honours your openness. Create a dance/string of movements which reflect going from weakness to strength, when entrusted to walk out with God, and in community.

WEAKNESS

INTRAPERSONAL

Ponder the areas of yourself, which are perceived weaknesses. How has God used these areas in you for something good? How do they impact your life? The lives of others? Your relationship with God? What part do they play in the whole picture?

VERBAL

Spend some time asking God what He wants to be for you in this time. With His help, craft a life declaration about what God has highlighted. E.g., "Even in my weakness, I am strong, because He is my strength. I am never without, because God is everything for me, that I am not."

INTERPERSONAL

Talk with a trusted friend or counsellor about God's nature and provision in the context of weakness and strengths. What role do they play in society? Talk about our need for one another in life. In vulnerability, be willing to share those areas which you are struggling with. Pray and declare trust in God to be what we are not.

NATURALISTIC

Observe the ways of weakness and strength in nature. How does one creature help another? How is one's strength help in another's weakness? How would it be if they didn't have one another? What would be the outcome?

Bless You

I bless you, trusted and much loved one, with a willingness to see yourself as He sees you.

I bless you with the ability to see any weakness as a strength when presented to Him.

Bless you…with fresh vision of Him where any weaknesses become opportunities for Him to shine in your life.

I bless you with courage to admit when you can't do it and to place your hand in His, choosing to trust once again.

Bless you…with His assurance that He has all that you need at this moment.

Be blessed with the understanding and experience of knowing that whatever you are not, He is and can be for you.

I bless you with the truth that weakness is not the end but can be the beginning.

Be blessed with the comfort of knowing that God loves our weaknesses. They can draw us nearer to our loving Father.

Bless you…with God's strength given to the weary and those who lack might.

I bless you with the knowledge that your power is increased through Him; as you wait upon Him, He will renew your strength.

I bless you with knowing that God doesn't expect perfection or strength, but an open and loving heart towards Him.

Bless you, with an expanded view of strength and weakness in life especially in this time of challenge.

In Jesus' loving, accepting, embracing of your name,

Amen.

xxxxx

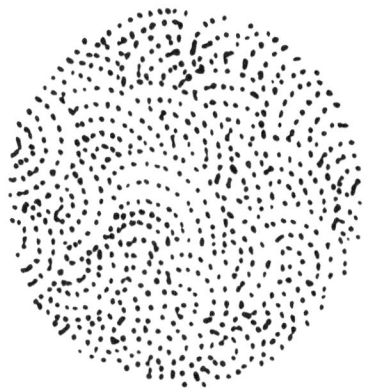

Chapter Fourteen

SMALL THINGS

— Father's Heart —

"It is in the small things that I am continually speaking to you.

Time and time again, I pour out My love over you, through those small things.

As you walk through your day and the worries of this world seem to pile upon you, the small things often get lost.

Yes, I can speak and work through the big miraculous things, but the heartbeat of Myself is that you might choose to sit with Me a while and enjoy the very things I have placed before you.

What do you have?

Look at your hand. What have I given you already?

Celebrate things such as these, My child.

I have placed along your path multitudes of joy gifts. They are all around you.

Wherever I am, there you will find My heavenly investments sent to light the spark I've placed within your heart.

You are hardwired for joy, My darling.

Ask Me to attune your sight, to foster an awareness of My gifts.

I haven't forgotten you; I see you. I know you. I long to lavish all these upon you.

I know the inner workings of the tiniest of sparrows.

See how I tend them? They do not lack anything they need.

Do I not care for you so much more than a sparrow?

Enjoy Me. Let's walk a while, and I will speak to you through things such as these.

In these small things I am revealed in the most intimate of ways.

I love you enough to share Myself with you—if you will open the eyes of your heart and keep watch.

You will begin to notice things that are all around you—the things I have placed to lift you and assure you of My love.

Give thanks for those small things, and you'll find your heart drawn closer to Mine.

Choosing to foster an awareness of those small things and gratefulness plants seeds of hope within.

Hope grows and flourishes, producing a significant impact on your current vision and circumstances.

These small things are actually life-changing.

The seemingly small things of life have enormous ripple effects. Those small things are hugely significant, beloved.

Becoming aware of the small prepares you for handling the big when it comes along.

Take heart, I am always at work for your good, encouraging and loving you, interacting in your life for your and others' good.

I do this because I love you and long for you to experience, respond to and embrace My love."

SMALL THINGS

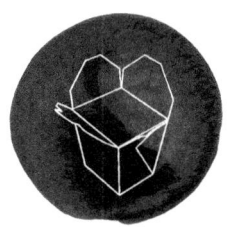

— *Take Aways* —

Small things, at their core, reinforce unshakeable faith in me. Truths like "God is good and is looking out for my and others' good always."

Small things are gifts from Him—both for us and for others.

GOD COMMUNICATES HIS MIRACULOUS LIFE RHYTHM THROUGH SMALL THINGS.

There can be greater value in 100 small things than 1 substantial something.

When added together, the small things in life make the most significant impact.

> Every day God is tenderly showing His great love for me through small things.

> As I align my vision to His sight, I find that small things are all around me.

> These same small things build in me faith for the BIG.

> The seemingly small things have often ended up being the most meaningful to me and having the greatest long-term value.

DON'T DESPISE THE DAY OF SMALL BEGINNINGS.

> Never underestimate the value of a strange or wacky idea—no matter how small. You might just be someone's angel from God, and they just might be yours.

SMALL THINGS

SMALL THINGS COUNT.

God desires for me to become aware of the many treasures He has placed all around me.

God places value on obedience—no matter how small.

Big things can be overwhelming and unreachable in hard times, but small things feel more achievable and possible.

Despite how I feel, I am all the richer for adopting the truth that small things are significant.

Small acts of obedience draw God's village together, and in love, we meet one another in relationship through them.

Small things build in me a greater awareness of my life having significance—despite my ability or capacity.

Small things are like God's stepping stones of pure love.

— *Questions to Ponder* —

1. Was there anything significant that jumped out for me in this chapter?

2. How present am I in the moment? Or, do I live futuristically, hoping that I was already in tomorrow?

3. Am I someone who is waiting for that one big thing to happen? Or, can I appreciate the small things along the way? Where do I place greater value?

> Are not two sparrows sold for a penny? Yet not one of them will fall to the ground apart from your Father. And even the very hairs on your head are all numbered. So don't be afraid you are worth more than many sparrows.
>
> **MATTHEW 10:29-31 NIV**

4. How easy is it for me to see and acknowledge the small things?

5. Does any part of me believe that God only does HUGE things, like parting the Red Sea and calming the storms?

> The Lord said to him, "What is that in your hand?" And he said, "A staff."
>
> **EXODUS 4:2 NASB**

SMALL THINGS

6. To what are my eyes attuned? Can they see the small for what they are? How will I steward these gifts? These ideas?

7. Is it possible that by being grateful, these small things actually grow to become larger blessings? Why or why not?

> And this is smaller than all the other seeds, but when it is full-grown, it is larger than the garden plants and becomes a tree, so that the birds of the air come and nest in its branches.
>
> **MATTHEW 13:32 NASB**

8. What would happen if I were able to appreciate those everyday moments as God gifts to me? What would happen to my thankfulness levels? What benefits might I experience in my mind, body, health, and spirit?

9. What if God speaks through the mountain-sized miracles, as well as the ant-sized? What if those small things are actually God's speaking to me in my current space? What is He saying to me through them?

> There is a lad here who has five barley loaves and two fish, but what are these for so many people?
>
> **JOHN 6:9 NASB**

SMALL THINGS

10. Challenges often keep us from being able to "do" much, but what if I am able to do something small? What advantages are there to acknowledging and valuing the small things in life?

It came about at the seventh time, that he said,
"Behold, a cloud as small as a man's hand is
coming up from the sea." And he said,
"Go up, say to Ahab, 'Prepare your chariot and go
down, so the heavy shower does not stop you.'"

1 KINGS 18:44 NASB

SMALL THINGS

— Small Things Playlist —

Oh Lord, You're Beautiful – Keith Green

Favorite Things – Sound of Music, Julie Andrews

Great Is Thy Faithfulness – Thomas Chisholm, Kansas, USA (1923)

You and Me – Lifehouse

Reckless Love – Bethel Music

His Eye is on the Sparrow – Lauryn Hill

Washed By The Water – NeedToBreathe (acoustic version)

— Activations —

MUSICAL

Create some lyric or instrumental music, which celebrate those small things which have had big impacts in your life. Times God met you in the small.

VISUAL

Is there something that you can celebrate today? Each day endeavour to look for at least one thing to be thankful for. Start a "small-things" calendar—mark off the small-thing observation each day. Take time to reflect on all that God has and is doing.

LOGICAL

Define *small things*. Small joys. Small but powerful. Meditate on Bible passages that talk about the power of small things. Notice the themes throughout. Where was a small thing offered, used, given, and a BIG flow of blessings resulted? What is the encouragement for me in these revelations?

KINESTHETIC/BODILY

Ask God to reveal someone you can bless. Even in the midst of tough, stepping out to do one small act of kindness not only can touch the receiver, but

SMALL THINGS

encourage us in our own space. If or when prompted, try doing one small act for someone else—a message, an anonymous gift in the mail, a token, a word, or something that God reveals. Go on a God adventure with Him.

INTRAPERSONAL

If there is power in small things, what are you more aware of today? Take a mental note of your thoughts, patterns, self-talk. Write them down as you notice themes. Then come to God and ask Him about them.

VERBAL

Spend some time listing the small things that often slip by unnoticed that God has placed in your life. You might consider people, places & provisions. What are those things that draw joy to your heart? What has brought the fruit of the Spirit to your life recently? These can be some of those seemingly small things that mean the world to us.

INTERPERSONAL

Consider the key people your heart loves most in your life. Take some time to recall those small but meaningful moments that you've brought one another in relationship. Spend some time in thanks for these.

NATURALISTIC

Go on a small-things hunt in creation. Today, focus on the small: The intricate-The details-The designs-The patterns-The colors. What do you notice? What do you see that reflects these? Thank God for them today.

CHAPTER FOURTEEN

— Bless You —

Bless you…one whose life is filled with God's goodness, big and small.

I bless you with a heart to see the value of the small things in life.

I bless you with a contented spirit and pace.

*Be blessed in seeing the significance of what God
has already placed in your hands.*

*Be blessed with seeing God grow what you
already have as you give it to Him.*

*Bless you…with the ability to see the small growing clouds
in the distance when all else around you seems bleak.*

*Bless you…with the thrill of hearing and
seeing God at work in your daily life.*

*Bless you…with a heart that praises Him when
He encourages you through small things.*

I bless you with eyes that keep watching for all that God is doing.

Bless you…with an ability to celebrate the small and the big wins.

*Be blessed as God reveals to you, in even more significant
ways, your personal and great worth to Him.*

In Jesus' intimate and hopeful name,

Amen.

xxxxx

Chapter Fifteen

PRACTICAL SURVIVAL TIPS

— Father's Heart —

"Be still before Me, My child, and I will give you rest (Matthew 11:28).

Life has required so much of you at times, and I can feel your exhaustion.

When you come to Me seeking refreshment, I do not expect you to push yourself beyond your limits. That is not what I designed for you.

Come to Me and learn the rhythm of My heartbeat. Learn My beat for you.

It will not look like anyone else's because I consider all the intricacies of your unique design.

My plan involves the best for you.

When My children live independently of Me, their lives become overwhelming and confusing.

When you walk with Me, I will whisper the truth for you.

I encourage you along the way.

I can show you the way of life and the way forward to freedom.

Let Me lead you, so our dance can release your heaviness, allowing you to float across the floor effortlessly.

As you know Me to a greater measure, the more you will see My truth.

*You were not created to always fit in this society but
to be counter-cultural on many levels.*

My Son is a perfect example of this.

He didn't focus on what was expected.

*Instead, in My love, He moved out, resourced
by My power, authority, and Spirit.*

He walked in joy, seeing the true nature of things.

I can give you those same eyes to see.

I can give you those same ears to hear.

*When you stop and rest with Me, I will show you your
best path. You will learn how we can flow together.*

*Yes, there will be hard times, but they will be seen
from My light-filled perspective of freedom.*

*There is a time for everything; seasons come and go, things move and
change. BUT, I am your constant. Unchanging. Solid as a rock.*

*Plant your feet on this rock, and you won't be shaken. You will
remain steadfast and sure, whatever comes your way.*

*Life will change. Routines, roles, and relationships,
all of these and more, can move.*

Place your trust afresh in Me, beloved. I am Your one truly secure place.

Come, let's walk a while, and I will give you rest."

PRACTICAL SURVIVAL TIPS

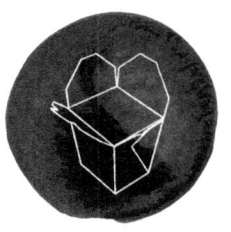

— *Take Aways* —

God has given me signposts—what I call life's checks and balances. These checks alert me to healthy and unhealthy ways of living well for my personal design.

Taking regular accounts of commitments is healthy for me.

God is inherently personal. I am uniquely designed by Him to walk through life as He knows is ideal for me. I was never meant to look, sound, or walk like another—only as myself.

My unique God design functions best when I ask the Creator how.

I don't need to be all things to all people.

- The things I did last season doesn't mean it's for this current season.

- My culture doesn't consider my unique God design. It often works against it.

- One person's health will be different from mine; no one is created like me.

- He gives me permission to be myself and shine as He created me to be. The world misses out if I spend my time trying to be someone else.

- Being healthy in all areas equates to being wealthy in my life.

- Saying yes to the best things is freeing and life-giving.

WITHIN THE CONTEXT OF INTIMACY, I ASK GOD FOR HIS LEADING.

- All opportunities are not always God opportunities. I am not designed to accept them all.

PRACTICAL SURVIVAL TIPS

Nothing is more saddening than to have a beautiful God-given opportunity come my way only to realize that I am too overscheduled, stretched, or exhausted to engage with or enjoy it.

Some come along to distract, detract or throw me off course from His best.

By neglecting or abusing my body, I dishonor God's creation.

My body is designed to send me signals; take note of the signs.

I honour God by taking care of my body, mind, and spirit.

Understanding what season I am in helps me to have a better life balance.

If I am healthy, those around me will benefit. Not everyone will be happy or comfortable with my setting new boundaries, but if they are God led, then it IS the best for me. Healthy new levels of relationship can ensue.

CHAPTER FIFTEEN

— *Questions to Ponder* —

1. Are there any parts of this chapter that seemed to be speaking directly to my heart? What aspects did I connect with?

   _____
   _____
   _____
   _____
   _____
   _____
   _____
   _____
   _____

2. Is comparison stopping me from shining in my own way before God?

   _____
   _____
   _____

PRACTICAL SURVIVAL TIPS

3. Do parts of me struggle in the area of worth? Identity? Ask God to highlight any areas He wants to renovate a little with me.

> This means that anyone who belongs to Christ has become a new person. The old life is gone; a new life has begun!
>
> **2 CORINTHIANS 5:17 NLT**

4. Can I see myself through God's lens? When I look at myself, do I see through a lens that highlights all that I am or what I am not?

5. Have I taken time to discover with God who I am? Who am I designed to be? Have I asked Him what He loves best about me?

> You were bought at a price, therefore honor God with your bodies.
>
> **I CORINTHIANS 6:20 NIV**

PRACTICAL SURVIVAL TIPS

6. Am I comfortable with the idea that I don't need to be all things to all people? Why or why not? What are my key relationships like? What would I like more or less of in the more challenging ones? What would bring greater health in this season?

---

7. Am I focused on old ways of being instead of what God has for me in this season? Eating old or new manna? Am I functioning in the old wineskins when God has a new one available for me? In what ways?

> I praise you because I am
> fearfully and wonderfully made;
> your works are wonderful,
> I know that full well.
>
> **PSALM 139:14 NIV**

8. Am I willing to let go of the old to be released into the life-giving new?

9. What does it mean to learn the rhythms of God's heartbeat? Moving forward, how would living this way impact my current situation and life? What advantages would reflection and action with God bring in life's checks and balances?

> Do you not know that your bodies are temples of the Holy Spirit, who is in you, whom you have received from God? You are not your own; you were bought at a price. Therefore honor God with your bodies.
>
> **1 CORINTHIANS 6:19-20 NIV**

10. What would be my next step in each area? (Refer to Appendix 6, page 353 as a reference)

Therefore, since we are surrounded by so great a cloud of witnesses, let us also lay aside every weight, and sin which clings so closely, and let us run with endurance the race that is set before us, looking to Jesus, the founder and perfecter of our faith, who for the joy that was set before him endured the cross, despising the shame, and is seated at the right hand of the throne of God.

HEBREWS 12:1-2 ESV

PRACTICAL SURVIVAL TIPS

— *Practical Survival Tips Playlist* —

The Creed, This I Believe – Hillsong

Turn Your Eyes upon Jesus – Helen Lemmel, England (1922)

Simplicity – Rend Collective

Head to the Heart – United Pursuit

Here's My Heart – Casting Crowns

New Wine – Hillsong Worship

— Activations —

MUSICAL

Ask God for insight into how your design flows best in this season. Explore frequencies, tones and melodies which lift your body, mind and spirit. Spend some time soaking in these sounds and praising God.

VISUAL

Pray for God to guide your heart as you look through magazines. Cut out anything that leaps out or that you are drawn to. When you feel finished, begin to put the main elements together. Create a vision board for this season. What is God showing you through the highlighted words and pictures?

LOGICAL

The parable of the ten virgins (Matthew 25:1-4) illustrates 'waiting well for God's best.' Reflect upon this story. Ask yourself, "What does the oil level in my lamp look like?" As you wait for God's leading, do you have reserves or are your levels depleted? What would change this in your own life?

PRACTICAL SURVIVAL TIPS

KINESTHETIC/BODILY

Consider how your body works best. What blesses it? What hinders health for you in this season? How does your body communicate that something needs adjusting? Do you take note of these messages? Bless your body in some way today.

INTRAPERSONAL

Ask God what you need for good health in this season. Refer to Appendix 6 for some further resource. You'll find some questions/ prompters. Spend some time talking to God about the areas of health. Ask Him to highlight any areas which need tweaking for improved health.

VERBAL

Write a persuasive piece that articulates the benefits of embracing your God design and walking forward in God lead health.

INTERPERSONAL

Meet with a trusted mentor or friend, pray for God's leading and then discuss the Appendix 6 questions/prompters. Be mindful of what aspects God highlights to you. Pray for one another. Set some action steps and accountability.

NATURALISTIC

Take a walk in a peaceful place in God's creation. Attune yourself to all that God is highlighting about the different areas of your life. Where are you thriving like the tropical forest? What areas are desert-like? Ask God to reveal your next steps.

— Bless You —

Most valued and precious one of His,

Bless you…with a greater awakening of all things kingdom.

I bless you with eyes to see yourself as He sees you.

*Be blessed with clarity about your identity—
knowing who you are and Whose you are.*

*I bless you with knowing the season you are in and
being able to rest in that revelation.*

Be blessed in freedom and permission to shine as you were designed.

Bless your heart with the security and assurance that can only come from Him.

*I bless you with personal acceptance and celebration
about your personality, design, and body.*

*Be blessed as you walk with the ability and confidence to step in
your own unique design and encourage others in theirs.*

*I bless you with clarity in your spiritual, physical,
emotional, mental, relational and personal health.*

*Bless your past, your present, and your future. May God bring you
increase in wisdom, discernment, and knowledge about how you
flourish in community, self, and, most importantly, with Him.*

In Jesus' personal, loving, encouraging name,

Amen.

xxxxx

Chapter Sixteen

VILLAGE LIFE

— Father's Heart —

"I have wired you for community, My child.

Just as I have my Spirit and My Son, you also have an intrinsic need for others.

Not one of you is complete in your own right, each having areas for others to enrich as you walk through life.

I have designed you for relationship.

You have something within you that is desperately needed by others.

This will not create something burdensome for you but will bring a richness to life that I designed from the beginning.

Understanding that you are needed by others and that you need others is the first step to capturing a glimpse of My perfect plan for humanity.

Just as I created Adam for friendship with Me, so too, I made you for friendship with Me—and in community.

You were made for interdependence—not independence.

If you find yourself lonely, isolated, or without community, ask Me for what your heart desires in this area. I long to give it to you.

After you ask, choose to be open to new friendships or rekindling relationships with old friends, discovering new depths within them.

Be open to accepting all people that I bring to your path and to being a friend.

Pray for like-minded and like-hearted people to come your way, and I will bring them. These are the ones who can be safe places to fall, the ones who encourage and lift. People who share your heart about the things I have impassioned you for.

These are the ones who will allow you to be yourself freely.

It is not only the ones who are like you that I design to be your village, but the ones who will sharpen you, challenge you, spur you on in greater measure towards Me. Not always easy, but always rewarding when it's walked with Me.

I provide a medley of people for you and your journey. They may not come in the package you expect, so remember to ask Me for confirmation.

I have surrounded you with individuals who long to connect.

You need to be mindful that, like you, others have areas that are still being refined. When you live with love in your heart and grace in mind, your village will be a fruitful and satisfying place to live.

Your village is not meant to replace Me but to enhance what I am already a part of. Healthy community will point the way to Me and My life-giving ways.

Be thankful for the people I have placed around you.

Encourage them frequently when you find yourself pondering how much they have lifted your life and made it better. Call out the gold in them.

Enjoy, bless, follow My leading, and I will bring you the right people at the right time to love and be loved by.

My plan is not for you to rely on one single person for everything.

Each one, being who I have designed them to be, can form a complete community. This will be my beloved church in its perfect wholeness."

VILLAGE LIFE

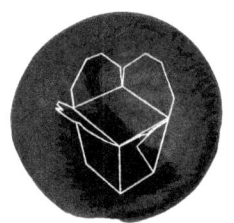

— Take Aways —

Every person on the planet is purposed for relationship—both with our Creator and with others. We are all in need of one another in life; friendships are the condiments for God's buffet spread for us. They bring out the richness of it, enhancing the flavor and "making" the meal so much more satisfying.

Having people that I allow "in" forms intimacy, growth, and depths within.

VILLAGE MEMBERS BRING A VITAL PART TO MY JOURNEY AND I TO THEIRS.

My village encourages me to see myself as God sees me, which has been an essential part of having hope in this season.

My village has been able to pinpoint the very things that I don't see and call them into being.

CHAPTER SIXTEEN

> When I choose to live independently, alone, and in control of all, I limit myself.

> Healthy village members are an integral part of walking in kingdom identity and crushing the insecurities of walking through whatever is served up.

> As we walk together in vulnerability, safety, and honesty in love, we can thrive as a "we," rather than just a "me."

> God designed me to hold only a portion of what is needed. By recognizing I have need, I am embracing the idea that God and others might have the vital parts that I need. And in turn, I might have something they need. Pure God poetry!

VILLAGE LIFE

I am confident that the enemy has endeavoured to crush healthy kingdom community, isolating people so they never actually find out that they are not alone in whatever they are walking through.

I AM DESIGNED TO BE A HELPER TO OTHERS—NOT THE SAVIOUR.

I am not alone. God has people waiting in the wings for me, and I for them.

Walking through the depths together means, in time, we can also walk through the joys!

My village should never become more important than my personal relationship with God. Him first, then others. During tough times, it's easy to become dependent upon people, but they are only one aspect of where my help comes from.

— Questions To Ponder —

1. Am I an island at times? Do I prefer to do it all by myself?

2. How comfortable am I with being vulnerable with others, sharing my life?

VILLAGE LIFE

3. What beliefs do I have about Christian community? Ask God about these views.

> All the believers were one in heart and mind. No one claimed that any of his possessions was his own, but they shared everything they had.
>
> **ACTS 4:32 NIV**

4. What have been my experiences of village life? Both healthy and unhealthy? What have I learnt from these experiences?

5. How has my village been evident in this difficult season?

VILLAGE LIFE

6. Do I understand my personality type? How does this relate to my interaction with others?

7. What part do I bring to the picture, Lord? What is unique about me that no one else can bring? How do these qualities or skills fit in this world? Ask Him for insight. It might be something brand-new. How do these relate to village life?

> Now you are the body of Christ, and each one of you is a part of it.
>
> **1 CORINTHIANS 12:27 NIV**

8. What are the ramifications if I am not functioning as I was designed? What are the implications if others aren't? How will I respond to the consequences? Is there anything I want to do or be different as a result? Ask God for the next step in this if prompted.

9. How do I best receive and give love naturally?

> I long to see you so that I may impart to you some spiritual gift to make you strong — that is, that you and I may be mutually encouraged by each other's faith.
>
> **ROMANS 1:11-12 NIV**

10. What advantages are there for life, when I can walk in mutual vulnerability with trusted village members? How does/could this impact my current situation?

* For those walking through a quiet or isolated village time-God hasn't forgotten you. Refer to Appendix 2.

May the God who gives endurance and encouragement give you
a spirit of unity among yourselves as you follow Christ Jesus;
so that with one heart and mouth, you may glorify the God
and Father of our Lord Jesus Christ. Accept one another then,
just as Christ accepted you, in order to bring praise to God.

ROMANS 15:5-7 NIV 1984

VILLAGE LIFE

All the People Said Amen – Matt Maher

The Blessing – Bethel and We the Kingdom

Que Sera – Justice Crew

Ain't No Mountain High Enough – Marvin Gaye

Leaving 99 – Audio Adrenaline

What a Friend We Have in Jesus

Speak Life – Toby Mac

330 CHAPTER SIXTEEN

— Activations —

MUSICAL

Write or compose a piece that reflects the thankfulness you feel about those people God has given you in your life. Sing a song of blessing over them.

VISUAL

Choose a puzzle to complete. Leave one piece to the side. Stop. Wait. Consider how this impacts the incomplete image. Reflect upon what happens when you are not functioning in your God design in the village. Place the last piece in position. Thank God for yours and others' unique design and personhood.

LOGICAL

Can you find biblical examples of village life? What kind of village did Jesus foster/experience with the disciples? With His family? Consider examples of village life working healthily and unhealthily in these times. What do these examples reveal about biblical times and now? What can be gleaned from these examples? What aspects would you like to give and receive from others?

KINESTHETIC/BODILY

For each finger on your hands, name one village member who has invested in you meaningfully. These investments don't have to be big; they can be small but significant to you. Thank God for the thing you value in them. Pray for them by name and bless them. (If prompted, send a quick note or message of encouragement to them.

INTRAPERSONAL

What parts of your personal design are areas of need? What are your areas of overflow? (Those things I find difficult or easy.) Who in your circle meets these needs in you? And you in them? Thank God for these perfectly placed friends and family members.

VERBAL

Write down some stories when God provided exactly what was needed through village members. Thank Him for these people and reach out to thank them both specifically and intentionally.

INTERPERSONAL

Spend some time thanking those people who have invested in your life. Bless them, as they have blessed you. Pray for them. Pray with them. Consider having a morning tea with someone.

NATURALISTIC

Consider how nature reflects the "village." Can you find some good examples of the village working harmoniously in nature? Think upon these with God.

— Bless You —

I bless you, valued one, with revelations of your great worth in this world.

Be blessed with an understanding of God's higher purpose of community in your life.

In this season, I bless you with an awareness of those God has placed around you as your village.

Bless you… with endurance, patience and provision from God that you would be made strong by being mutually encouraged by one another's faith in your village.

Be blessed as you navigate people, relationships, and needs.

Bless you… with knowing that you are an essential part of a larger picture, no one is meant to do this alone.

Bless you… with the revelation that healthy people give and receive.

I bless you with the freedom to know what you need now and to ask for it.

Be blessed with knowing that God knows what you need in this very moment.

I bless you a firm reliance upon God to provide—even in the times when it feels like your village is absent.

I bless you with a grateful heart for those God does place along your path.

Be blessed with an expansion of your ability to see who you have in your hand right now.

Bless you…with a oneness of heart and mind as you and your village learn to share what you have.

I bless you with hope, with love, and with faith to take the next step forward, however small it might be.

In the powerfully loyal and fiercely loving, community-hearted name of Jesus,

Amen.

xxxxx

APPENDIX 1

Rest for me is *not*:

- Busy
- Chaotic
- Noisy
- Confusing and lacking the ability to think.
- Finding it hard to hear Father God's voice
- A consistently full calendar
- Wrapped up in activities and distractions
- Whining, groaning, or lack focused
- Having so many commitments that leave no time to breathe
- Task-based
- Being absent or elsewhere
- Overwhelming
- Listening only to what society demands
- Burdensome or heavy
- Doing it all myself/ independence
- Self-reliant
- Distracted and anxious

What is rest *not* for you?

Rest for me *is*:

- A place of "being" rather than "doing"
- Being present and in the moment
- Where God can be heard/sensed loud and clear
- Where God has a chance to have my full attention
- When my entire being is refreshed and restored
- Where God's peace reigns
- Where the big questions of life are asked and answered
- When moments of great discovery and revelation happen
- Healing, restorative, and always refreshing

- Where fresh perspective is given
- Leaving space and time in the calendar for God
- Asking God what He thinks, rather than accepting what is provided by my surrounding circumstances
- When I become aware of my body and the incredible systems at work
- Connectedness in vulnerability and authenticity with God
- Healthy dependence on God and those He has placed around me
- Where intimacy with God is developed
- Relational and personal
- Peaceful and calm
- A starting point for everything in life

What *is* rest like for you?

APPENDIX 2

Village Life

For those walking through a quiet village time—a walking-with-God time

— Take Aways —

Social isolation is HARD.

If I stay in this mindset, it will not add anything good to my life.

Asking whether I can do anything to find my village and taking actions is well worth the journey.

Despite how I feel, I am not alone.

God can be all things that I need when others aren't available.

God's desire is for me to have community.

I commune with Him first; others may follow.

People WILL let me down; they will not meet my expectations 100 percent of the time. They are on a healing journey as well.

Talking with Him about my frustrations and needs releases heaviness from me.

Giving grace and forgiveness to those who have neglected, hurt or injured me will allow me to fly more freely and lightly in this tough season. Holding on to past hurts weighs me down and often the other person is unaware of the consequences of their actions.

Becoming with God who and what I desire from others is a fabulous desire of my heart, e.g., if I desire encouragers in my village, am I encouraging?

I am not forgotten.

I am valued.

I am worthy of having a village to interact with.

Sometimes God is working something in me, knowing that this time of process needs to be just He and I.

Coming to peace about His being my only friend is challenging but also a place of rest.

He knows what and who will bless me at this time.

Sometimes I am hidden because He is protecting my heart.

My own expectations of village sometimes need realignment. Asking God if my beliefs about community align with His is a rich journey to go on.

My view of who and what I need can be different from what God KNOWS I actually need. Be willing to travel this path with Him, openly vulnerable. He won't lead me astray.

Fostering thankfulness for what and who I do have already can springboard me into a different headspace and life view.

VILLAGE LIFE

— Questions to Ponder —

1. What kind of village do I want in life? What type of village do I have?

2. Is there a gap? Am I willing to ask God for what I need?

3. Is it possible that God wants to tweak something in me at this time regarding the village He has given me?

4. Looking back, can I see seasons where I have walked just with God? Have there been other times where I have walked closely with others?

5. How comfortable am I with seasons in life? What helped me get through those quieter village seasons?

6. What benefits will come from this time alone with God? How could this bless future village life?

VILLAGE LIFE

— *Activations* —

At times, what we think we need in our village seems absent. This void can be an isolating and grievous space. Sometimes I have felt completely alone in this world, and it's no sweet place—until I meet Him in my depths.

> Spend some time talking to God about this void. Process any grief or disappointment with Him.

Talk to Him about what people He has given and what each is bringing. Ask Him what things He wants to be for me in this season. Talk to God about what He is growing and developing within me during this season.

> If I am in a season without the village I envisioned, it's time to ask God some questions.

> "What season am I in, Lord?" Sometimes we walk alone in order to rely upon and find our answers in Him.

> "Who have You already given me?" (Even if they aren't what you imagined having.) Sometimes the perfect village in hardship is shared across ten people instead of just one.

Then we can ask some self-awareness questions: "Is there something in me that needs tweaking?" Subconsciously we can sometimes push people away that God has provided for us. "Have I been doing this, Lord?" If so, why? "Am I always asking things of others, or do I bring something to them as well?" "Have I invested in others?" "Have I shared my need with them?"

"Am I sharing with safe people? Letting others in? Or keeping them at a distance?"

Create something that reflects how you feel when God brings the perfect person with His provision. What happens to your heart? Express this in some form.

APPENDIX 3

Safe Places, Safe People

Jesus...

- was *loyal* in His relationship with the disciples. Romans 12:10, "Be *devoted* to one another in brotherly love; give preference to one another in *honor*."

- was *unselfish*, choosing to offer Himself as a sacrifice that we might live. 1 Peter 3:18, "For Christ also suffered once for sins, the righteous for the unrighteous, that he might bring us to God, being put to death in the flesh but made alive in the spirit."

- was *generous* throughout His life with His time, energy, and resources. Acts 20:35, "In all things I have shown you that by working hard in this way we must help the weak and remember the words of the Lord Jesus, how he said, 'It is more blessed to give than to receive.'"

- was *compassionate* and *kind-hearted*, especially with the weak, broken, and needy. Matthew 9:36 (NLT), "When he saw the crowds, he had compassion on them because they were confused and helpless, like sheep without a shepherd."

- was *wise*. When visiting the temple as a boy, He impressed the educated priests (Luke 2:46-47).

- was *thoughtful* in his care for Mary and Martha. Luke 10:41-42, "Martha, Martha," the Lord replied, "you are worried and upset about many things. But only one thing is necessary. Mary has chosen the good portion, and it will not be taken away from her."
- *saw the heart* of each person and *didn't judge* a person by what others said, e.g., Zacchaeus (Luke 19:1-10) and the woman at the well (John 4:1-40).
- *spoke the truth in love* when He gently chastised Peter.
- Was *self-sacrificing* in the best way, sometimes choosing to minister to others even though He was tired, e.g., the woman at the well (John 4:1-26).
- was *encouraging* when the disciples were fishing (Luke 5:1-11).
- was *merciful* as He healed countless suffering people, including the ear of the arresting Roman soldier (Luke 22:49-51).
- was *comforting* in His support of Lazarus's sisters and His sorrow at the death of His friend. John 11:33 (NIV), "When Jesus saw her weeping, and the Jews who had come along with her also weeping, he was deeply moved in spirit and troubled."
- *modeled the practice of rest* and displayed *healthy boundaries* when He went to a quiet place to be by Himself. Luke 5:16, "But Jesus often withdrew to the wilderness for prayer."
- didn't tolerate things that were not aligned with God's heart when He drove the sellers from the temple. He *stood up for what was right* before God (John 2:13-17).

APPENDIX 4

Be Kind To Myself

When being kind to myself, a few areas might need tweaking. Take note of any words or phrases that jump out. This may be God's prompting you to take your next step. Take note of your body responses and thoughts that pop into your mind.

1. Rest & meditation
2. Time with God
3. Eating well for my design
4. Adequate regular sleep
5. Relaxation or down-time.
6. Cutting the chaos out of the calendar
7. Sculpting some spontaneous time into your day or week
8. Community: Quality time spent with loved ones.
9. Exercising
10. Journaling
11. Seeing a counselor to broach past/present troubles.

12. Reading life-giving words from the Bible often

13. Getting some alone time

14. Fasting the things that draw energy from you

15. Connecting with a church community regularly

16. Understanding technology's place in my life

17. Keep short accounts.

18. Participate in activity that energises.

Consider the areas of care and ask God to highlight the areas—spiritual, physical, mental, emotional—that could use some tweaking in this season. Now formulate some next steps with Father as you walk forward in a healthier you!

APPENDIX 5

Listening Foundations

- Consider this idea a good friend once shared with me: "There are three voices we hear after asking God something. The first voice/thought is God, full of hope, encouragement, and life.
- The second voice/thought is the enemy sending doubt, i.e., words that come in direct opposition to what God has said.
- The third is often my own voice reasoning it all out."
- Make a mental note of being more aware of when God might be speaking to me. Start small and then increase awareness with practice.
- If you are unsure whether it is God, take some time to test it out. Ask God for something for someone else, then give them that word. Does it reflect His loving nature? Is it supported by Scripture? Does it reflect any of the fruits of the Spirit?
- When all else fails, or if you can't test it with others, I have endeavoured to live by the truth, if it's encouraging and good, and then go for it! If it reflects His heart and the fruit of the Spirit, jump in! What's the worst that could happen? Yes, you could be wrong, and at the very least, you will have interacted with something good. But at the most, you could have heard from God Himself, who wants to bring You goodness, especially amid times of trouble.

APPENDIX 6

Life checks and balances

God has been teaching me throughout this season of health struggles about the importance of looking after myself. We may put ourselves last, especially as servants of the kingdom. Still, God tells us to care for ourselves as temples of His Holy Spirit (1 Corinthians 6:19). He has revealed how I am to do this in several areas of reflection. As you read through the declarations and questions, what areas is God highlighting to you? Take note of them.

PHYSICALLY

I have discovered how my physical body thrives.

I am blessing my body with the amount of sleep I know it needs.

I eat healthily and have good nutrition.

I remember to drink lots of water and remain hydrated throughout my day. I engage in a balanced amount of appropriate exercise.

I remember to go outside often into the fresh air.

I try to remain mobile, even on the tougher days.
Every bit of movement helps.

LIFE BALANCE

What does my calendar look like?

My priorities are reflected in my calendar.

Have I reflected with God about my commitments? Are there things that God has equipped and impassioned me for?

I am choosing to bless my body with a lifestyle that pleases God.

Are there fresh things that God is calling me to?

Am I willing to let go of things that are no longer a part of my current season?

I ensure that my God-given life priorities are reflected in my week, e.g., family, work, church, rest, and health.

I take time to regularly reassess things with God.

I ensure that amidst all the serious things of life, there is still the fun factor!

My calendar will make room for the spontaneous and God adventures that He invites me into.

EMOTIONALLY

How are the stress levels in my life?

Do I need to process some situations that have occurred?

Do I need to allow God to heal some parts of me?

Do I need to forgive someone or something?

Am I able to care for myself and my family well? Or do I need help?

I can check the outside reality and allow God to reveal what is happening internally.

Am I self-aware? Do I question what was my part when
things go pear-shaped? Or do I blame others?

How do I rectify this and seek peace and pursue it with people?

I understand my God-given design and how I best thrive emotionally.

I know to give to others but also how to receive from others.

I have healthy people around me who are good for me emotionally.

I keep check of my emotional health.

On tough days I give myself grace.

I realize that a moment in time does not need to steal the entire day.

MENTALLY

Am I able to enjoy something in life?

Do I experience joy?

Is my thought life investing health or stealing it from me at the moment?

I understand that trouble comes, it's what I do with it that matters most.

I give myself permission to seek help if I need it. I do this
without shame or condemnation. I do this because sometimes
we all need a helping hand to get through a tough time.

Do I need some professional help with the processing of circumstances?

I am strong when I acknowledge my need for help and take steps to obtain it.

I am worth the investment of time, energy, and money
when it comes to good mental health.

How does God see me at this moment?

I have a growing intimacy with God that helps me to be healthy mentally.

I readily observe what things I tell myself through the mind and can assess whether they are for my good.

I can come to Father at any moment and ask for clarity or revelation about my current circumstance.

RELATIONALLY

I will set healthy boundaries in relationships.

I will talk to God about life and stressors.

I will endeavour to surround myself with good friends who are healthy and life-giving.

I will ask God who my inner circle of friends should be.

I will not adopt problems that are not mine to carry.

I will not care more about other's problems than they do.

I will keep my emotions in check and endeavour to be authentic and loving when I have injured others, or they have injured me.

Am I investing time in the people and things that really matter to me? Am I relying upon God to be my best friend and source, rather than having unrealistic expectations of friends who are also on their own journey of healing?

PERSONALLY

How do I operate best? How can I flourish? Who have You created me to be, Lord?

If I am stuck, I have researched my personality type and gone on a journey to discover who I am in God.

I know what fills my tank.

I understand the things that deplete my oil levels.

I can celebrate my unique God design.

I find it easy to set healthy boundaries.

SPIRITUALLY

Am I talking with God and listening for what He is saying throughout my day?

I regularly engage with/in His Word, the Bible?

I set aside time to rest in God.

I connect with God through thanks.

I understand that everything can be spiritual, and, in this context, nothing is outside or apart from God. Daily tasks, relationships, work, study, sleep, these and more can be a place or an opportunity to connect with Father.

I am free to fly with Father God, as I put my hand in His and journey through life together.

ENCOURAGEMENT FOR THOSE ON A
Spiritual Journey
WHO WANT TO CONNECT WITH GOD FOR THEMSELVES

Firstly, welcome; thank you for picking up my book.

You could have taken a look at countless books; I'm thankful that you landed here. Whatever it was that led you here, I am confident that it's no mistake. This page is just for you if you are on a spiritual journey and want to know more about and encounter God for yourself.

No doubt, God has some encouragement for you—yes, even in your own challenging time. He loves all people, and the good news is that it includes us both. You've read some of my experiences with Him through this book, and no doubt you'll have your own to share as well.

If we met in everyday life, we'd probably be sitting down with a cuppa and having a good conversation about life, faith, and whatever else came up.

We'd possibly share about our tough seasons and our challenges, but also the incredible things—those unexplainable moments which can only come from something outside of ourselves—that have happened along the way. These kinds of encounters are exciting to hear and to talk about with one another.

I'd be celebrating your unique God design and cheering you on in your journey. I love nothing better than doing this with whoever God brings along my path.

I know that you'd leave having been encouraged by Him, and I'd feel blessed for having met you. Although I appreciate your being here and taking a bold step forward in faith and exploration, this obviously isn't our meeting in person, which got me to thinking, *How does this happen through the pages of a book? How do I encourage someone I might never meet or talk with? What advice would I give to those who want to know God for themselves?*

So I began asking God for some advice. What steps do I take that have helped me connect with Him best? He answered me through a dream, and I wrote down the five steps He showed me.

1. BEGIN.

When I say *begin*, I mean start asking God to speak in a way that you understand.

Start talking to Him about everything. If you have questions, ask them.

Nothing is off-limits when it comes to talking to God.

Talking to God can be implemented through speaking verbally, journaling, or thinking with Him. Our "hows" do not limit Him, He is more interested in connecting rather than how you choose to connect with Him. Rest assured, He wants to be heard as much as you want to hear Him.

2. FOSTER AN AWARENESS OF HIM.

Keep watch, wait and take note of what He is saying, showing you, and how you sense His communicating with you in the everyday.

Some of the ways He speaks are found in this book series, but there are soooooo many more. Chances are, He has already been talking to you. You might not have recognized that God's voice doesn't necessarily sound like a Morgan Freeman voiceover, mystical, loud, or booming.

His voice can be the voice you hear in the quiet—the gentle prompting. Or when you feel your heart respond to something, this can be His Spirit leading you.

If you've ever felt or experienced love, joy, peace, kindness, patience, goodness, hope, or any other life-giving aspect, this IS God speaking. Without Him, these virtues would not exist.

Has something drawn your eye? Has something out of the ordinary happened? God is often in these too.

Nothing is off-limits when it comes to how God can communicate with you. Take note of those times when you are tended to, encouraged, or lifted. These kinds of help bear the heart of God.

Once you start noticing Him and taking note of His voice, you'll see He is always present and speaking with you.

3. START READING.

Get yourself a Bible or use a bible app. Plenty of options are available; I have found YouVersion is a great resource.

Start with the book of Mark. It talks about the life of Jesus, and none of this means anything without Jesus.

When exploring online, a plethora of options are available. How do we navigate this with wisdom? I find it's healthy to ask questions about anything I read:

- Is what I'm reading reflecting Jesus' heart and nature?
- Is it supported by the teachings of the Bible?
- Does it draw me closer to God and a healthy relationship with Him?

If it does all these things, then you are off to a good start.

4. FIND YOUR KIND OF PEOPLE.

We all need one another, so look out for and connect with a healthy local church or Christian community where we can grow together and encourage one another.

Ask God to show you where to start.

Understand that most churches differ in terms of worship styles and some beliefs. It's good to find one which fits how God has designed you to connect with Him.

5. CHECK OUT THE ALPHA WEBSITE.

This site (alpha.org.au) is a safe place to ask all those nagging questions and to wrestle with the significant issues. It's also an excellent resource for further information about Jesus and becoming a Christian.

God doesn't require you to work or strive to be loved by Him. He doesn't require you to be good enough to have a relationship with Him. He naturally wants to reveal Himself to those who want to get to know Him.

He's incredibly personal and wholly relational, and best of all, whether or not you know Him, He loves you 100 percent. Nothing you could do will ever change this unconditional love of His. It's great news!

I will be praying that your spiritual journey will be the best adventure of your life.

However you choose to take the next step, know that He is closer than you think, cares about you and all that you are going through, and has ways for you to flourish despite circumstances.

I hope you will thoroughly enjoy getting to know Father God in the way He has planned for you. I know it'll bless your life; I know this because I've lived the truth of it for decades. Woah, that makes me feel really old. Lol! But it's true!

God bless you, precious one; I'll be praying for you.

xxxxx

ABOUT THE AUTHOR

Karen Brough is an Australian wife, mother, writer, and former primary school teacher. She is the author of the *Be Held by Him* series, *Finding God* when life knocks you off your feet.

Ten years ago, when hit by a mystery illness, Karen began sharing the encouragements God gave her via her blog: *writtenbygodsgirl.com*.

Her unique voice makes her readers feel understood, inspired, hopeful and encouraged. She spurs others on to connect with Father God for themselves by sharing the adventures she has with Him in everyday life.

Karen has always had a passion for writing and for encouraging others and cannot remember a time without this. Her blog has been read and enjoyed both domestically and internationally over the past eight years.

She loves nothing better than to spend time with her husband and three children. In warmer months, you'll often find her at the beach body boarding or lying by the pool doing crosswords and creating "healthy" gelato for anyone who might be dropping by. She finds herself telling the family groodle Gracie to "get out of the vegetable patch!"

In cooler weather, she loves baking anything warm, comforting and delicious—often hiding vegetables in sweet muffin recipes, much to her children's disgust. (Secretly they love it though.)

She loves the slower, unhurried pace of life and following this past health challenge season, desires God's peace above all else. She loves to laugh, cry and love with her whole heart and wants to leave this earth a whole lot better than she came into it.

BOOK WEBSITE: BEHELDBYHIM.COM
FACEBOOK: BE HELD BY HIM
INSTAGRAM: BEHELDBYHIM
WRITTEN BY GOD'S GIRL: WRITTENBYGODSGIRL.COM
KAREN BROUGH: KARENBROUGHAUTHOR.COM

We'd love to hear from you!

Has something spoken to you or your situation?

Is there a particular quote which touched your heart?

Do you have a testimony of His goodness in your own hard time?

If you have any encouragements, fan art or inspirational creations that might help inspire or affirm others, share and connect with your online village on the

'Be Held by Him' facebook page

or email us at **beheldbyhimseries@gmail.com**

GOD BLESS YOU DEARLY, BRAVE ONE.

Next in the series:

Subscribe for the latest information at **karenbrough.com**

www.ingramcontent.com/pod-product-compliance
Lightning Source LLC
Chambersburg PA
CBHW071953290426
44109CB00018B/2009